FEEL GOOD

A Holistic Roadmap

Live Your Life
Love Your Life

BHADA SINHAPHALIN

You can only find true happiness if all the elements are aligned. If you are in balance, emotionally, physically, you can find your inner strength.

I loved how Bhada explains the different techniques available, and that he gives the option for readers to follow whatever suits them best. As we are all unique, this is the way to move forward. I like the tone that is not imposing, but reaching out and wanting to help others by explaining his path. His positive message that it is possible to reset the brain and that anyone can change their way is compelling.

It is a beautiful book that many will enjoy and that can help improve lives. In our fast-moving and changing society, where many have lost the human connection, it is an essential message.

What Bhada describes about finding your passion is what happened to me when I arrived in Sumba, Indonesia, and started my project. The contradiction of a beautiful place and extreme poverty was shocking to me, coming as I was from a completely different environment. I just felt I had to do something. How could I make my life more meaningful by sharing my skills and experience? I built a project where I combined all my passions. All the pieces of the puzzle finally fitted: all the things I did before in my life, courses I had followed, my hobbies, and people I had met through the years came together in that one project. Being flexible and open for change is the key to success.

Inge De Lathauwer, Founder of the Sumba Hospitality
Foundation, Sumba, Indonesia

Bhada is the Feel Good Man, from defying life-threatening illness to changing the world with his book. He's living proof that Feel Good X works.

With FeelGoodX, Bhada shares his life values, his suggestions for emotional health, and a real book for everyone.

Mr. Johnson Wong, Chief Operating Officer, Plaza Premium
Group, Hong Kong

This book is a gem. Concise and easy to read, it provides that holistic roadmap we all have been eager to discover and follow.

It encompasses so much, yet with such a natural delivery. It is logical but filled with the emotion of real-life experiences and thoughts that Bhada has had and lived. The backgrounds and beliefs he shares have been the building blocks of his road map.

The uniqueness of his book is that it is also a philosophical essay. It is a book on how we live, our mindsets, relationships, culture, and sense of purpose. Beyond being didactical, it has a far-reaching human touch—the touch of a man known for his sensitivity and his quest for betterment.

The book can be opened at any page or chapter according to one's interest. Each part provides a great read on its own, covering the theme and applying purpose at the same time. It is a book that will stay with you always.

The many quotes Bhada makes from worldly individuals and references to their actions give consecration to his discipline. It gives us so much to think about, and we are grateful for it.

Mr. Gerard Sintes, General Manager, Hotel Ritz, Madrid, Spain and Area Vice President Operations, Mandarin Oriental Hotel Group

FeelGoodX is required reading for those who seek to live a balanced and fulfilling life. From his own experience of personal transformation, Bhada shares his observations, insights, and wisdom to guide us through the eight elements of FeelGoodX.

Starting with Emotional Heath, I found myself on a personal journey of self-discovery and awareness of what I needed to address in my life to become a better version of me. FeelGoodX is for today!

Dr. Ross McKenzie, Entrepreneur, Founder & CEO of The Startup Business, Sydney, Australia

Everyone loves to feel good. Instead of offering a superficial solution, Bhada packages it so well with a holistic approach on what matters most. He discusses each subject in depth: health, relationship, environment, and many more, sharing his wealth of experiences along with what experts say. I enjoyed the stories. My personal favorite is the discussion on Purpose and how he advocates to "break up with the ONE."

Ms. Michelle Liew, SVP, Head of Group Customer Experience, RHB Banking Group, Kuala Lumpur, Malaysia

Inspirational, motivational, and beautifully written, FeelGoodX is an enlightening read for people of all ages.

Bhada offers pearls of wisdom about multiple aspects of life that are often overlooked and underestimated.

He shares the very best of his experiences in his pursuit of a meaningful and fulfilling life.

FeelGoodX encourages you to stop and smell the roses and is sincere and helpful in its teachings of self-understanding.

Dr. Dennis Kwan, Medical Director, Dermacare Aesthetic & Laser Clinic, Singapore

First published by Silverfish Books (2019)
for FEELGOODX PTE LTD (201932898C)
FXP is an imprint of FEELGOODX PTE.LTD (201932898C)
Website: silverfishbooks.com, e-mail: info@silverfishbooks.com
FEELGOODX© Bhada Sinhaphalin (2019)
First print: 2019

Disclaimer:

The author, copyright owner, and publisher, respectively, have made their best efforts to produce this high-quality, informative, and helpful book. They have verified the technical accuracy of the information and contents of this book. However, the information cannot replace or substitute the services of trained professionals in any field, including but not limited to mental health, nutrition, medical, financial, psychological,or legal fields. They do not offer any professional, personal, medical, financial, or legal advice, and none of the information contained in the book should be confused as such. Any information pertaining to the events, dates, and other details relating to the person or persons, dead or alive, and to any companies have been verified to the best of the author's abilities based on information obtained or extracted from various websites, newspaper clippings, and other public media. However, they make no representation or warranties of any kind with regards to the contents of this book and accept no liability of any kind for any losses or damages caused or alleged to be caused directly or indirectly from using the information contained herein.

Cataloging-in-Publication Data

Bhada Sinhaphalin, 1964-
FEELGOODX: LIVE YOUR LIFE, LOVE YOUR LIFE / BHADA SINHAPHALIN.
ISBN 978-983-3221-92-9
1. Self-actualisation (Psychology).
2. Motivation (Psychology).
I. Title.
158.1

Published by Silverfish Books Sdn Bhd (483433-K)
20-2F Bangsar Village 2, Bangsar Baru, 59100 Kuala Lumpur, Malaysia.

Printed by Image Printec (M) Sdn Bhd
221-222 Jalan Negara 2, Metro Melawati, 53100 Kuala Lumpur, Malaysia.

Table of Contents

This book is dedicated to the generous and purposeful souls, old and young, who are determined to live and love their lives and be part of communities.
Thank you for enjoying the journey, not just the destination.
I promise to create a world with you in which we make every day a masterpiece.

Introduction

I used to think that to "feel good" was to have a good career and earn a lot of money. That was my belief during my younger years. Luckily, in my search for the "real" feelgood, I found it. This book is about my personal journey from not knowing the meaning of "feelgood" to becoming a man with FeelGoodX. The X is for extra. And no one is more surprised than I am that I wrote this book about how to feel good all the time.

If I can do it, then, truly, anyone can.

As teens, we were given all kinds of tutoring to guide us as emerging adults, but we receive none of this same tutoring as emerging elders. Most people above 50 feel they are over the hill. I didn't like those odds, so I adopted what Tony Robbins calls a "growth mindset", determined to be different from the status quo. I discovered the real meaning of "feeling good" on my own, using various means such as listening to podcasts, attending seminars, and joining online courses. With my newfound knowledge, I started to embrace this new mastery while appreciating the roles of both a wisdom keeper and a seeker.

Some parts of this book tell of the experiences of friends or former colleagues, but most of what I share here are my experiences alone. What happened to me is unique to my circumstances. I hope this book will give you some inspiration that FeelGoodX is not hard and requires only your determination to find your new path. What happens to you will be unique to you.

Practice makes perfect, but nobody is perfect. There is beauty in how our practices differ. Noticing and honoring what is easy and difficult for you will support your journey much better than blindly following exactly what I did.

My experience is a barometer by which to gauge your own situation, along with the FeelGoodX library of quotes, manifestos, checklists, and charts provided throughout this book. Once you have your bearings, take from this guide whatever you want. Make FeelGoodX your own, and share it with others through our website and Facebook. With this, you will have something that stays with you for your entire life, and a new tool of joy to lead your life. None of that can be taken away from you.

May your FeelGoodX journey be successful beyond your wildest dreams.

FEELGOODX

LIVE YOUR LIFE, LOVE YOUR LIFE

Let's begin

"I choose to make the rest of my life the best of my life. "
—Louise Hay

This book is designed to encourage a mind shift towards greater relevance, and to empower you to consider what's next for your wellbeing road map. Because life is a trip. Modern life is a two-tank journey. Society's outdated model of a three-stage life (Learn, Earn, Retire) taught us this was a one-tank ride where we fuel up with curiosity and counsel in our Learn period (mostly our teens and early 20s) and burn most of our school fuel in the Earn period. But today, with the increased longevity and accelerated changes of the modern world, many of us are running on fumes and in need of a midlife pit stop.

I consider myself to be in midlife. And let's face it, midlife is a marathon. For the past half a century, since the phrase "midlife crisis" emerged into popular lexicon, midlife has been defined as 45-65 years of age. But today, in many industries, geographies, and cultures, people start feeling "old" in their mid-30s. And on the other side of the spectrum, with an increasing percentage of us living to 100, it is plausible that midlife might extend into your mid-70s. This new timespan from 35 to 75 feels like a run-on sentence that could use a little punctuation.

Midlife hasn't historically come with any kind of societal rituals, other than the stereotypical gold coin (or any form of gold) after spending decades in the same job. Yet midlife is full of stressful transitions—whether it's marriage, divorce, career changes, or caring for children or aging parents, midlife is a time of exhaustion from the sheer volume of identities we inhabit.

The increased longevity we may have, compared to our parents or grandparents, doesn't necessarily mean an extra ten years tacked onto the end of life. Rather, it means we have an extra decade in our midlife. When I left my position as a senior executive in hospitality a few years ago, I started pondering how those of us in midlife could create a new architectural blueprint for our lives: not by slapping an addition onto the back, but by creating a bright hall in the centre. The hall is filled with fresh air and sunlight, and it presents an opportunity for reflection on all the rooms that open off it, inviting us to discover a variety of choices about how to spend our extra years.

To build the bright hall, we must have a purpose in life. Sharing our unique gifts with the world allows us to tap into more joyful living. Why are you here? What is your calling?

This concept is so deeply connected to our lives—spiritually, emotionally, and even physically. In fact, research has shown that having a sense of purpose produces longer, happier lives. Having a greater purpose in life is consistently found to predict lower mortality risk, and the longevity benefits of feeling a sense of purpose are apparent even after other indicators of psychological wellbeing, like relationships and emotional status, were accounted for.

Discover your purpose

So how can we tap into our own sense of purpose? Here are the top three tips that have helped me find my own calling and live a fulfilled life:

Notice what makes you feel best. The expression, "If you do what you love, you will never work a day in your life" holds true. It is useful in discovering what I am really passionate about, along with what unique skills I am able to offer the world and how these skills can benefit others. This applies to all phases of my life. What did I love as a child? What activities were drawn to throughout school? As an adult, what parts of my schedule did I look forward to the most? These are all helpful clues that led me to feel a stronger sense of purpose in how I interacted with the world so that I could begin formulating a plan to do great things.

In with the good, out with the bad. Take a close look at your normal routine. Is it packed with obligations and things you do not truly enjoy? Is all your free time devoted to doing things for other people, while the activities you want to do fall by the wayside? Finding your purpose means nothing if you don't make regular time for activities that support it. Early on, I started saying "no" to things I found draining, and filled my time with things that sparked my passion. I got rid of the distractions that were sucking away my precious time. I skipped many hours of TV and social media and went to bed earlier, so I could wake up earlier to tackle projects that energised me. I prioritised the things that ignited me and made me feel alive. Doing this more frequently is a sure-fire way to feel more meaning throughout life.

Be open to possibilities. You may have more than one purpose in this life, so it's important to realise how all of your different passions can co-exist and become something truly special. Anything is possible! For me, the first step was owning who I am, pursuing what I cared about, and allowing myself to seize the opportunities that brought me a feeling of purpose.

It is never too late to tune into your sense of purpose and identify ways to strengthen its role in your everyday life. Start with these simple tips and reap the mental, spiritual, and physical benefits as you embrace your passions.

My purpose

Many years ago, I went through a life-threatening and difficult period. I had to change what was on my plate and be open to new things, such as meaningful spiritual practice, enjoyable physical activity, an inspiring career that I love, and honest and open relationships. I am lucky to have my wife to support and encourage me in this new journey.

I started the journey with finding my own "why," like who I am and what my main goal is. Without that, my "what"—like meditation every morning—would not stick with me. My initial goal was for myself, and now many years have passed, I am aiming to lead a movement to inspire everyone to find their own "why."

I like Simon Sinek's golden circle concept from his book *Start with Why*. The golden circle consists of three concentric circles, with the "why" as a bull's-eye in the centre, the "how" wrapped around that, and the "what" as the outermost circle.

For "how," I have come up with the term FeelGood. FeelGood is nourishment that doesn't appear on the plate. When why, how, and what are balanced, food is secondary. I discovered that healthy relationships, regular physical activity, a fulfilling career, and a spiritual practice could fill my soul and satisfy my hunger for life. By nourishing myself on a holistic level, I feel more vibrant with joy, meaning, and fulfilment.

The modern mystic Osho said, "To be in romance with life is religion." Osho did not teach any religion or belong to any affinity. He believed that when we create nourishing lives for ourselves, *that* is the highest form of religion. Osho's neutral, holistic approach to life and religion mimics the core of FeelGood. Osho said that the body needs physical food, of course, but taught that a robust, fulfilling life is the real fuel for happiness and balance.

Of course, my journey of FeelGood needed adjustment, and I had to make changes that, at the time, were intimidating. I believe that we should face our challenges anyway. Along this journey, I embarked on a new career, ended any relationship that was no longer serving me, and learned new skills, like the fundamentals of wellbeing, that aren't typically taught in schools.

After a few years, I found that a fulfilling career, loving relationships, an energising and rejuvenating exercise routine, and a spiritual practice were not all that I should include in my FeelGood. I continue to search, always taking the next step to bring myself closer to complete mental, emotional, spiritual, and physical satisfaction.

There were many missing elements that would infuse more joy and satisfaction into my life. The new additional elements included:

Part A: Heart

Emotional health

Purpose

Part B: Health

Food

Body and movement

Finances

Home and environment

Part C: Soul

Mindset and practices

Relationships

From the list, I looked for the "how" to find the way in which the "what" is achieved: how do I handle everything? What is it that, for example, turns my financial process into something more structured and beneficial to me and my family?

My "why" is to "live my life, love my life." The "how" are those elements that I listed above. And the "what" are those actions that I do to achieve each element.

Want to be successful? Feel good first! When we experience positive emotions, the feelgood chemicals *dopamine* and *serotonin* flood our brains. These chemicals give us more than good vibes; they also boost the parts of our brains responsible for learning.

It's no surprise, then, that psychological studies have found that when we feel good and have a positive mindset, our brains work better and we feel more motivated, which leads to more success.

In fact, over 200 happiness studies involving nearly 275,000 people found that it's *happiness* that leads to *success* in nearly every aspect of our lives—from relationships to jobs, and from health to creativity.

We can learn a lot from this. We just need to practise feeling good in the moment, perhaps through meditation or mindfulness. It's also a great excuse to do more things that delight and relax you! It'll set you up for a successful future.

When I set out for FeelGoodX, I began with goals. I applied what I learnt from an interview that Larry King did with Carl Lewis, an American track and field athlete who won nine Olympic gold medals. King asked, "What advice do you have for people pursuing dreams?" Lewis' reply was, "Start with the ultimate and work back." This is the mindset of the great achievers. They have a clear idea of what they want in their lives, and they develop a "backwards plan" to get it. If I don't know what I want, it is hard to know how to make decisions in day-to-day life. But if I have a clear picture about what I want in my life, I can measure my daily decisions against my ultimate goals. This helps me plan all the little intermediate steps that I need to take along the way, and makes my goal feel real in my head. It changed me from a dreamer to a doer, and from someone with a wish to someone with a plan.

PART A: Heart

LIVE YOUR LIFE,
LOVE YOUR LIFE

FEELGOODX

Emotional health

As human beings, we are constantly told that something is missing in our lives, and that buying a certain product or going on a special holiday will make us whole. There are many things that we have been programmed to think we need because society has told us who we are and what we are supposed to want. We like to think that modern human beings are a clever and highly rational bunch. But the truth is we tend to make a lot of our decisions based on the emotions we feel at any given moment, which means we are often pretty irrational. Actually, this struggle between our emotional and rational sides has been going on for ages.

Envy affects our emotion. We do have envy in our nature, but many don't like to admit it. The saying goes, *The grass is always greener on the other side of the fence, and there is always a better place just over the horizon.* In fact, we are competitive by nature and feel a strong desire for things if we encounter them in the real world or in our imagination. However, if we admit to the fact that everyone has these feelings, we can start putting them to work for us.

When I was young, I would sweep my emotions under the carpet and refuse to deal with difficult feelings that came up. I did not want to create conflict with my loved ones and, truthfully, I did not want to create conflict internally. My childhood was based on my parents being too involved and preventing me from establishing my own identity. This resulted in low self-esteem and feelings of insecurity. Luckily, it was not deep enough to create patterns of jealousy, attention seeking, taking everything personally, and being unable to handle criticism. It did, however, cause me to become aggressive. After I acknowledged the reason, I managed to achieve a healthy level of aggression and find ways to put it to good use. We all have some level of aggression in us. Our aggressive nature helped make us the dominant species on the planet. What I did was stop repressing this part of my personality, as that would lead to passive aggression. Repressed anger can also show up as an internal voice that projects the aggression inward, toward the self.

Each and every one of us has a mix of strong and weak qualities. Some of these qualities we gain genetically, while others are from our upbringing. Then there are the ones we pick up later in life. For me, I created a sense of self much later in life, which reduced insecurity and raised self-esteem. Slowly, I look for how to process my emotions with grace and wisdom. The process has been extremely beneficial, and it has made me realise that emotional intelligence is a powerful ally in creating better health and wellness. This is due to our innate traits not being a prison: we can control them, and even weak ones can be used to our advantage. No matter the cards we have been dealt in life, we can strive to be of superior character. That is why I place emotional health at the top of the list.

One of my weaknesses is being defensive. Everyone is defensive to some degree, because everyone privileges autonomy and free will. However, after reducing my natural stubbornness and learning to show appreciation to others, while validating their individuality and intelligence, I can say that I have almost overcome that.

I also discovered that, to perform at my best, I need to recognise my tendency to neglect the big picture in favour of immediate concerns. First, I need to take a step back when making decisions and calmly consider the problem at hand, what my options are, and what the consequences are likely to be. Sometimes, doing nothing is the best thing to do! I like that both Japanese and Chinese cultures recognise the strategic wisdom in waiting to see what happens and in letting the enemy wear himself out. In the past, I used to think doing nothing was a sign of weakness. Now I know better.

I have spent many of my happiest days clouded by anxiety because I have been waiting for the other shoe to drop. I had to relearn the simplest things, like how to just enjoy a moment for what it is without worrying about some impending doom. I learnt to trust myself more instead of panicking about everything that could go wrong. It is not easy, probably because I allowed a feeling to take control of me. There was comfort in familiarity and justification, even when it was rooted in a negative experience. But ultimately, I realise that holding onto the past has no real benefit; it only holds me back from achieving my true potential. Before, I used the past to justify my current decision-making, and that is why I did not want to let go. When I was unable to let go, that became a part of my "story" that worked against me, holding me back. Luckily, I found the answer by asking if I was willing to change my story.

Letting go is not as hard as it may seem. Bad things happen, sure, but I cannot change the past, so why continue to perpetuate it? The key to letting go of a painful past experience is that we have to face what has happened, accept that we can't change it, and then move on. Once I am able to move on and close old doors, inevitably new doors will open up, better opportunities will arise and, most of all, I will have a better story that moves me forward instead of holding me back. My key point is to start writing a new story today.

I like The Beatles and the simple song "Let it Be" has helped me scratch the surface and realise the profound beauty in just letting things be what they are. It is through letting go that I can finally bid farewell to my anxiety and learn to see this life in a new light, one that is not controlled. It is a life in which I allow things to happen as they do and land just where they are meant to land. It is a life in which I finally learn to surrender, and with surrendering I can be peaceful and free.

Moreover, with the dark side of my personality, whether it is negative feelings or just selfish impulses, the first step is to acknowledge it. Then I can begin to use it in positive ways. Stepping into our feelings with vulnerability, love, and kindness can help turn our emotional compass into a friend instead of a foe. That is because the more we push the bad feelings away, the more power they seem to hold over us.

Emotion is a powerful tool, and our mental state greatly affects how we perceive the world. Consider, for example, how negative emotions skew our view of other people: when we are angry, even dear friends can seem annoying, cold, and hostile.

> **"Let your mind guide your emotions, not the other way around"**
> **—Jonathan Landsman**

According to the Dalai Lama, it is possible to systematically train your mind so that you can cultivate positive emotional and metal states while eliminating the negative ones. This is very difficult for me to achieve. It is a slow, gradual process, but I believe it will eventually bring a calmness that allows me to live a happy, joyous life, no matter the external situation.

The teachings of the Dalai Lama place great emphasis on developing and cultivating compassion. It is an important component not only of Buddhist spiritual development, but also of robust, lasting happiness.

I didn't have much compassion in the past. It took me a long time to understand what compassion is. Compassion can be roughly defined as a state of mind that is non-aggressive; it's a wish to see others free from suffering. In true compassion, this wish is deep, not related to personal feelings or attachments to particular people. Rather, it applies to all living creatures, including friends and enemies. I am still on the journey to cultivate compassion. I have found an effective method for this is to understand their backgrounds and focus on the commonalities we share. Say, for example, someone tries to cheat or be mean to me; instead of getting angry, I think about what that person and I have in common, like the fact that we may both be tired, hungry, etc. Then, I try to picture myself in their shoes: how would I feel? This usually helps me develop empathy and reduces the anger I would feel, leading to more compassion and a happier life.

Another important ingredient of good emotional health is spirituality. My belief is contrary to what many people think spirituality is not dependent on any specific religion; however, it is well documented in numerous studies that a strong religious conviction can lead to happiness and better health, and any major religion can offer people the opportunity for a happier life.

Basic spirituality can be practised in everyday life without prayers or mantras. For me, if I find myself tempted to insult someone, I practise basic spirituality by challenging that wish and restraining myself from indulging in it.

In fact, there is also a kind of spirituality that exists outside of the sphere of religious belief: basic spirituality comprises basic human qualities like goodness, compassion, and caring for others. Embracing these qualities brings us closer to all of humanity, helping us become calmer, happier, and more peaceful. In short, though religious beliefs can be beneficial to happiness and emotion, we can cultivate basic spirituality without them.

Suffering is an inevitable part of life, but I often increase it unnecessarily. When I do encounter suffering in one form or another, my mental attitude becomes of paramount importance. I have found that if I fear suffering as something unnatural and unfair, I will feel like a victim and assign blame when I should instead be trying to eliminate the root causes of suffering.

Suffering may be natural, but I often inadvertently magnify it by actively subjecting myself to unnecessary anguish. For example, I often resist change and cling to the things I care about or possess. But change is a constant, and resisting it will inevitably result in more suffering as I lose the things I have clung to.

Living in Bangkok, Thailand, has made me accept the fact that suffering is a universal and perfectly natural part of life, perhaps because I live closer to poverty and daily suffering than those who live in developed countries. The fortunate tend not to understand that suffering is a part of life, and often see themselves as victims of some malignant force when something goes wrong. Another common source of unnecessary suffering is hanging onto past negative events, mentally replaying them and perpetuating the pain. By accepting that suffering is natural, I can confront and analyse its causes, including whether I may be partially creating it, and then begin to lead with more positive emotions and a happier life.

I continue with determined efforts and frequent reminders to eliminate negative attitudes, feelings, and habits. Anger and fear are obstructions that stop me from achieving my natural, happy state. I have discovered that certain positive states of mind— love, compassion, patience, generosity—can act as antidotes, eliminating harmful emotions, attitudes, and behaviours. Hence, I am fully aware that I need to eliminate negativity, and that positive emotions and behaviours should be habitually cultivated.

So far, the process of habituation has taken me many years, and expectations of a "quick fix" are unrealistic; however, through similarly determined efforts and frequent reminders, I, too, can eventually establish new behaviours.

When I encountered a negative situation, I used to see it very rigidly, as 100% negative, even though most situations contain both positive and negative elements and can be viewed from several alternative angles. For example, I might have considered having to face an annoying person as a purely negative situation, or I could see it as an opportunity to practise patience and tolerance. The important part is to acknowledge the dark side of my personality, and to begin to use it in positive ways.

Such a switch can help me find meaning in suffering when I next encounter obstacles in my life. I no longer wallow in self-pity and say, "Why me?!" Instead, I consider it a chance to become stronger. I find purpose in suffering and thrive.

The ability to shift perspectives is facilitated by having a so-called supple mind, or a certain mental flexibility. We can all develop this flexibility by deliberately trying to shift perspectives as we encounter unpleasant events in life. People with supple minds may be seen as indecisive and inconsistent because they don't abide by a rigid value system. My solution is to reduce my value system to its most basic principles that can be applied in a vast array of daily situations, rather than adhering to specific rules that might be unnecessarily constraining and inappropriate in some cases.

I keep practising. It takes time and effort to see the good in negative events when they occur. Just as a tree cannot grow strong roots at the last minute to survive a storm on the horizon, it has taken me years to decide on the meaning and purpose of illness in my life.

Our emotional state is affected by the negative mental states of anger and hatred. When a feeling of anger or hatred arises in me, it rapidly destroys my peace of mind. It also obliterates my judgement, often leading me to take actions that only worsen the situation and make me even angrier.

Anger and hatred cannot be overcome by simply suppressing them. On the other hand, venting anger, such as through raging and shouting, tends to increase negative feelings, not reduce them. I have learned to use patience and tolerance against these feelings, and to cultivate them through meditative exercises. Since anger tends to arise from a mind that is discontented, I try to build a mindset of inner contentment, which is very difficult. But studies have shown that stress decreases the threshold of feeling anger, which means that reducing stress by cultivating calmness and contentment can help reduce feelings of anger.

As much as possible when I feel angry, I take a time-out: I pause to analyse the situation, notice my anger, and try to replace negative feelings with thoughts of patience and tolerance. As a result, my anger often recedes.

Affective emotions—our jealousy, anger, hatred, and fear—can be part of us. When I realise these emotions are only temporary, that they always pass like clouds in the sky, I can ultimately be a better person by not letting them affect me and the people around me.

From time to time, I experience anxiety and worry. The sources of anxiety are many. Recently, I have come to favor a Japanese tool of dealing with them. It is called Morita therapy, created by psychotherapist and Buddhist Shoma Morita. Originally, he developed it to deal with chronic anxiety, obsessions, and compulsions; however, it also works great on stress and burnout.

Unlike some western therapies that focus on using thoughts to influence feelings and actions, Morita therapy takes the opposite approach.

We assume that we must "overcome" fear to dive into the pool or make a public presentation. But, in actuality, it is not necessary to change our feelings in order to take action. In fact, it is our efforts to change our feelings that often make us feel even worse.

In Morita therapy, we are asked to pay attention to and accept the feelings without attempting to change them. Acceptance of reality as it is involves accepting our feelings and thoughts without trying to change or "work through" them. This means that when we feel depressed, we accept our feeling of depression. If we feel anxious, we accept our feelings of anxiety. Rather than direct our attention and energy to our feeling state, we instead direct our efforts toward living our life well. We set goals and take steps to accomplish what is important, even as we co-exist with unpleasant feelings from time to time.

For me, excessive anxiety is often related to poor self-confidence. Probably the best way is to be honest with myself about my capabilities and limitations. Once I feel comfortable with my own limits, I can confidently admit when I cannot do something or do not know something, and not lose my self-esteem by doing so. On the other hand, if I feel that I am up to it, I switch my thoughts and motivate myself to go for it.

Emotional wellness is connected to all areas of life. Let's stop running away from our own feelings and start embracing them with courage. Our bodies will thank us with health!

My number one rule for emotion is that when I control my emotions, I control my game.

Emotional health is about more than navigating social interactions. It's also about understanding our own emotions, and strategising around that awareness. These inward dimensions of self-awareness and emotional discipline can seed both personal and professional success.

Emotional health is an overall understanding of how to engage with others, as well as an awareness of their possible emotions. Therefore, yes, emotional awareness and emotional discipline are parts of our work. For instance, if I tend to feel annoyed or angered by anyone, it is important to label the feeling, to understand the triggers for this emotion, and to learn how to manage it when engaging with this individual.

Emotional health means understanding people, including ourselves.

It's a miscalculation to assume that the intensity of our feelings is a strategic basis around which to shape our behaviours. "I feel it, therefore I owe it to myself to express it" is not a savvy way to operate. It's understandable to feel stressed, mad, frustrated, disappointed, or worried. But rather than indulging these raw emotions, it's a sounder strategy to work through the feelings, use Morita therapy, and reframe them.

To be emotionally disciplined means to recognise how to handle different emotions at different times. For instance, if I am receiving critical feedback, while it may be upsetting, it is important to know that it may not serve me well to respond in an angry manner (e.g., become defensive, storm off, or cry). Emotional discipline allows me to respond appropriately to the expectations of the setting and the audience, to make the impression I wish to make.

Enacting emotional discipline is a practiced skill, and it can be especially helpful for all of us. Part of emotional discipline is to model suitable behaviour. For instance, during a crisis, people around us may not want us to appear overwhelmed or out of control.

This may seem like a lot of emotional processing. The key here is to explore and understand the feelings, and to do this work at times that suit us. Having an emotional outburst doesn't make anyone seem sincere or well grounded.

Another helpful tip is to be strategic about when I plan difficult conversations. I think through when the best time for these discussions is before I head home for the day or week. Whenever possible, I aim to position difficult conversations at times when they're more likely to land softly.

I always cultivate calm and clarity during moments of tremendous pressure: I am convinced that being fully committed to the moment, without any worries about the past or projections into the future, is the best attribute a closer can have.

Emotional health manifesto

In any situation, regardless of how difficult it may be, I will exhibit strength and control. I will display the courage to stand steadfast in my principles, even in the face of impossible circumstances. I will take these words to heart:

> External circumstances cannot create lasting happiness; the right state of mind can.

> Cultivating universal compassion is a way to a healthier, happier life.

Though religious beliefs can be beneficial to emotion and happiness, I can cultivate basic spirituality without them.

Suffering is a natural part of life, but I often increase it unnecessarily.

I can eliminate negative attitudes, feelings, and habits only through sustained effort.

I must be able to shift perspective and find the good in every situation.

I confront and analyse my feelings of anger and hatred, and replace them with patience and tolerance.

I combat anxiety and low confidence by examining my thoughts, motives, and capacities honestly.

> *"You have to apply yourself each day to become a little better. By becoming a little better each and every day, over a period of time, you will become a lot better."*
> —Coach John Wooden

FEELGOODX
LIVE YOUR LIFE, LOVE YOUR LIFE

Purpose

Efforts and courage are not enough without purpose and direction.
—John F. Kennedy

For decades, psychologists have studied how long-term, meaningful goals develop over the span of our lives. The goals that foster a sense of purpose are the ones that can potentially change the lives of other people, like launching an organisation, researching disease, or teaching kids to read.

Indeed, a sense of purpose appears to have evolved in humans so that we can accomplish big things together—which may be why it's associated with better physical and mental health. Purpose is adaptive, in an evolutionary sense. It helps both individuals and the species to survive.

Many seem to believe that purpose arises from your special gifts and sets you apart from other people—but that's only part of the truth. It also grows from our connection to others, which is why a crisis of purpose is often a symptom of isolation. Once you find your path, you'll almost certainly find others travelling along with you, hoping to reach the same destination—a community.

Do you feel lost or as if something is missing in your life? Maybe you want to make a bigger difference in the world than you feel you are right now, but you aren't sure how. So many of us walk through life feeling numb and desperate for a deeper connection, but we aren't sure how to get it.

Mark Twain once said, "the two greatest days of your life are the day you were born and the day you find out why," but if you don't know what your purpose is, then you don't know why you are here, and it can be hard to keep going.

I know this feeling all too well. I used to suffer immense inner turmoil while trying hard to find my purpose. I was in a job I hated, working in a corporate office under fluorescent lights, and suffocating from the stale corporate air. I saw Beyonce shine so brightly when she performed or Roger Federer so energetic when he played. I wanted what they had: infectious passion, a thirsty love for life, and an unyielding connection to their work.

I struggled daily to figure out my purpose, but as Bob Dylan once said in an interview with *Rolling Stone*, "Everyone has a calling." For me, it wasn't until I took a step back and realised that my purpose isn't just from my head that I found a way to get there. I thought to myself, *Maybe the problem isn't that I don't know what my purpose is; the problem is the way I am trying to find my purpose.*

On days of frustration, I question why I have not figured it all out. On days of reflection, I ponder what serves me. On the good days, I feel that purpose in my bones. On the bad days, I feel no purpose at all. It is normal to have an occasional "off day," but if I'm regularly struggling to be motivated, then I know that I have missed a life purpose.

I know that I have to tend to my mental garden, and the best way to take care of it is to stand guard at its gates. Only let pleasant, positive thoughts in, and ban the detrimental ones. At the end of the day, our thoughts shape our lives. I would have a better standard of living if I filled my head with worthwhile thoughts. Want to live a peaceful, meaningful life? Then let the peaceful meaningful thoughts in! But how do we get our minds to focus solely on fulfilling thoughts? Well, we all have the ability to choose what we think about, so it all comes down to exercising our minds like a muscle.

In Sanskrit, the word *"dharma"* means *"life's purpose"*. *Dharma* comes from the ancient belief that, while on earth, we each have a mission to complete. By honouring *dharma*, I can achieve lasting satisfaction and inner harmony.

Webster's Dictionary defines purpose as, "something set up as an object or end to be." "End to be" sounds like something out of our control because, at the end of the day, we will end up at our truest destination, and life is just trying to figure out what that is along the way. Mega achievers such as Bill Gates and Jeff Bezos are filled with incredible passion and purpose. They know what they want in life, and they are driven to get it.

What if my life's purpose is to be present here on Earth because my life's mission is determining what serves me and what I am willing to contribute? Without purpose, I've found it is hard to stay motivated, and a lack of passion hinders the natural flow of life.

I like the book *Man's Search for Meaning* by Viktor Frankl, an author who survived the Nazi concentration camps and reflects on how prisoners found purpose and meaning in life. Viktor Frankl said there is no general meaning of life; every life has its own specific meaning in a given moment. Knowing how important it is to find a purpose in life, we are left asking ourselves how we go about finding our own. Indeed, many people believe that, in order to make the right choices in life, they must first discover their life's purpose.

For example, the prisoners in the concentration camps who were able to maintain a purpose in life did so based on the choices they made. The decision to look for beauty in nature or help others in greater need gave them a purpose, a realisation that they were not beaten and could keep going.

> *"Those who have a 'why' to live can bear with almost any 'how.'"—Victor E. Frankl*

Our meanings don't have to be the same. In fact, everyone has their own meaning of life. The chess Grandmaster knows that there is no best move in general. There is, however, a best move depending on the varying situations during the game. The same applies to life: there is no general meaning of life, and life's meaning depends on each individual's unique set of circumstances and decisions.

With clear vision to picture my future, I can proactively create my life in accordance with my desire. One source of inspiration for me is Malala Yousafzai. Even though she was shot by Taliban members for her beliefs, she refused to give up the fight for education rights for girls in Pakistan. Her vision of changing women's lives for the better was too compelling for her to just stop.

After years of facing issues and difficulties, I have come to understand that no matter what has happened to me over the course of my life, I have the awesome ability to choose how I respond. When tragedy strikes, if I am not aware of my purpose, I can easily become a victim of circumstance. By living on purpose, I have a reason beyond circumstance to continue, despite the worst of the worst. To endure hardships, I connected to my inner power, strength, love, and compassion. Without having an open mind and a curious spirit, I could not discover my purpose and experience all the great stuff that comes along with that.

The fact is, no matter what I have been through, someone else (and most likely millions of other people) has already gone through it or is going through it right now. My problems, my past, my hurt, and my trauma are not what make me special. What makes me special is my ability to discover and thrive in my purpose despite all those things.

We all have a powerful, resilient, infinite, unstoppable spirit within us. To access it, I have to get out of my own way, and decide that from this moment forward, I am going to devote time and effort to achieving results and creating the outcomes I truly desire. The secret is to love whatever I do or have, make it meaningful, and be grateful for every moment that I can help another person.

For a long time, I did not know my purpose. I knew I wanted something more from life, but I was not sure what, and I was struggling. When I first began working toward uncovering my purpose, I landed on something very general by attending various seminars, listening to podcasts, reading books, etc.

My purpose today is to share writing and coaching that is packed with value, truth, inspiration, encouragement, and hope. That is pretty specific, and because of that, I know what the most important things are to accomplish. I fix my eyes on the finish line and then I can run toward it all day—writing, researching and learning, taking awesome care of myself, coaching, and working on my business. To start, I created a mental image of the outcome and placed pressure on myself, but in a good way. Pressure can be a wonderful source of inspiration, as it can often push a person to realise their full potential. A great way to generate pressure is to tell others about my plan. From there, I constructed my timeline to get my goal underway. I must have a deadline in sight. I keep doing this until it becomes a new habit.

> **"Failing to plan is planning to fail. What are your goals?"**
> **—Brian Tracy**

For the same reason you have never seen a bored marathoner or race car driver, you won't see me with ennui. I am motivated. I am doing what I love and working toward my dream of making a bigger difference, and I know exactly how I am going to do that. We are all here in this world for a reason. If I don't live my purpose, it can be painful. I know because I was there, living an unfulfilled and unhealthy life. But once I step into my purpose, life becomes incredibly joyful and abundant as I make this world a better place.

The key takeaway from this is that our core values/principles provide purposes/goals. It is important to be realistic about how to plan to achieve them and not to get caught up in a distraction.

Consider the principle of nonviolence, which Nelson Mandela believed. When it proved ineffective in bringing down the brutal apartheid regime, he abandoned it. It was not his core principle. Once Mandela emerged from prison with the aim of finally ushering in a democratic and socially equal society, he did not get distracted by abstract models like socialism, capitalism, or tribalism. He stands for implementing key social change, with equal rights and opportunities for all.

As long as we stick to our core values/principles, we can adjust our purposes to changing conditions for pragmatic reason.

We can't *think* our way into our life's passion and purpose; we have to *do* our way in. This means taking steps towardŏ what you want, and removing those things in your life that you don't want. I left my successful corporate job on a mission to find my happy, and it came by taking one step at a time and exploring many different passions. If you are looking for your purpose and passion, stop looking and start doing. These steps that helped me will help you.

How to find your purpose and passion

Take more action. You can't think your way into finding your life purpose; you have to do your way into it. Take a mental note from Nike and Just Do It. The more we act, the more we get clear on things. So instead of overthinking it—*Will this work out? Should I try that? What if I don't like it? What if I don't make money at it?*—start taking steps toward your goals, and start trying new things. This will help you get out of your own way. I struggled for years trying to find out what my purpose was. This cycle only created a deeper lack of clarity. It wasn't until I started doing that things changed for me. The experience is the reward; clarity comes through the process of exploring. Action is where you get results. We can use the sumo wrestler philosophy called *kaizen*, a Japanese word that means constant, never-ending improvement. It is all about unlocking your potential. Remember this: self-mastery leads to life mastery. You practice *kaizen* by pushing yourself daily.

In the movie *The Pursuit of Happyness*, a 2006 American biographical drama based on entrepreneur Chris Gardner's one-year struggle being homeless, we learned the importance of taking action.

> *"You got a dream. You gotta protect it.*
> *People can't do somethin' themselves, they*
> *wanna tell you you can't do it. If you want*
> *somethin', go get it. Period!"*
> *—Chris Gardner*

You have a choice to be stuck where you are and keep complaining, or take your life in your hands, decide where you want to be, and no matter what is happening here and now, keep moving towards your goal. See the clear steps. Don't look around or back, and don't let others' success or troubles make you doubt yourself.

Drop from your head to your heart. Your heart is your best tool to access your true purpose and passion. Ask yourself what you love. Then start taking steps to do what you love. When you are inspired and connected to your happy self, inspiration floods your heart and soul. When you lead from your heart, you are naturally more joyful and motivated to explore. By doing what you love, you will be inspired and gain insights into what brings you the most joy. Therefore, it is important to use your time efficiently and plan how to spend it. Think that time mastery is life mastery. We have to believe that we should always live life to the fullest. It is important to learn to say no. Live each day as if it were your last— that way, you won't end up wasting time agreeing to an activity that you don't want to engage with. It helps to ask yourself, "Would I want to spend my last day on Earth doing this?"

Break up with the "ONE." Many of us struggle because we try to find that ONE thing that we are meant to do, but trying to find only one thing is the reason we feel like something is missing. The notion that we have only one thing we are meant for limits us from fulfilling our greatness. Take me, for example: I have multiple different job titles. I'm a health coach, hospitality consultant, author, speaker, and investor, and each thing I do brings me joy, but none of these are my purpose. They are my passions. So start getting in touch with your passions! When you lead a passionate life, you are living your life on purpose.

Let go of thinking there is only one purpose for you and embrace the idea that our purpose in life is to love life fully by putting ourselves into our life! This means we jump in and try new things; we stop resisting the unknown, and we fully engage with what is happening right here, where we are. To lead a purposeful life, follow your passions. When we live a passion-filled life, we are living on purpose, and that is the purpose of life.

In any good teaching, we know that we should always be kind and compassionate toward others, as it improves our own lives. An ancient Chinese proverb says that a trace of fragrance always remains on the hands that present you with roses. The roses stand for the concept of selflessly serving others. Take a moment every morning to think about goodness you can spread in the world and how you can better the lives of other people. It can be as simple as sincerely praying for others, helping your friends when they are in need, and showing affection toward your family. Behaving in such a kind, earnest way will lead to a happier way of life. I believe that by having a personal journey, you can give your life a sense of purpose, especially if your quest is directed toward a greater cause.

Mr. Richard Hatter, my ex-boss of some 25 years ago, shared a story with me that he grew up as a "third culture kid." He made it his absolute priority to always give back to the community and ensure that opportunities were available to ALL, regardless of gender, race, ethnicity, or country of origin. While he was not directly responsible for training, he always committed himself to grooming the mid-level managers to take on more senior roles.

The feeling that something is missing goes away when you lead a passion-filled life. The need to seek our purpose comes from a lack of passion. When you don't feel connected to your life, you lack purpose and passion. To fix this emptiness, simply add more passion. To boil it down, remember this simple equation: Passion + Daily Action = Purposeful Life. The key is to "live in the now" and understand that a purposeful life is not the destination, but the journey itself. Because ultimately, the journey itself, not just the end result, will bring you more self-fulfilment, happiness, and a better life.

Consider that the real purpose of anyone's life is to be fully involved in living. Try to be present for the journey and fully embrace it. Soon you will be radiating passion, and you will feel so purposeful and fulfilled that you will wonder how you lived life without it. Enjoy the journey into your own awesome life.

For more inspiration on purpose, you may want to watch some films. In particular, I like these two movies: *Groundhog Day* accurately conveys the perils of living every day without any difference. It gives a strong message when it comes to seizing your life and changing it. *The Devil Wears Prada* is another insightful movie about the expectations of ambition, kindness, and finding a purpose in this world.

I also use music to help, and this song is my most favourite. "It's My Life" by Bon Jovi is a very empowering, optimistic song. The interesting thing about the song is that it has appealed to me across time, from my younger days to now. I can understand the essence and feel good when I hear it.

> It's my life
>
> And it's now or never
>
> I ain't gonna live forever
>
> I just want to live while I'm alive
>
> (It's my life)
>
> My heart is like an open highway
>
> Like Frankie said
>
> I did it my way
>
> I just want to live while I'm alive
>
> 'Cause it's my life

PART B: Health
LIVE YOUR LIFE,
LOVE YOUR LIFE

FEELGOODX

LIVE YOUR LIFE, LOVE YOUR LIFE

Food

"I can't control everything in my life, but I can control what I put into my body."

Have you ever attempted a diet, only to fail miserably? If you are like most people, the answer is yes. The worst part? It often leaves you feeling a sense of moral failure, as if you weren't good enough or strong enough to attain the body and health you deserve.

You aren't alone! This phenomenon was very publicly on display in an article on 31st October 2017 by Gina Kolata in the *New York Times.* The article featured contestants from the TV show *The Biggest Loser.* All of them experienced dramatic weight loss during the taping of the show, then regained that weight shortly after the cameras went away. One thing is becoming abundantly clear: the billion-dollar diet industry does not work. We have been badly misled when it comes to healthy eating and living.

Fortunately, there are simple ways to keep ourselves in good shape and excellent health.

After having experienced many types of diet, including being vegan for five years, I think it is better to have a diet based on FeelGoodX's key ideas and core principles. It is a way of life, not a diet. A diet is just a short-term commitment, and it will always be missing something very important. FeelGoodX focuses not only on food, but on many other components. It will have a big influence on the quality and duration of your health and life. My goal is to create a ripple effect by making changes to our relationships with our body, feelings, habits, and food. The food program is designed to break old habits in three weeks, develop new habits in six weeks, and codify it into your life in 36 weeks.

> *"Every single person in the world, every culture, every language, every country, you are what you eat. Food does matter."*
> *—David Wolfe*

What are the core principles of FeelGoodX for food?

One specific diet for everyone does not work. Everyone has different needs, processing capabilities, and nutritional requirements.

Food that comes from plants is better for your health. The further away a diet is from plant-based, the greater the chances are that it will create disease or a weakened immune system. Factory-created food is all about marketing campaigns and addictive ingredients that are designed to get people to eat far more than they really need. Don't take food that offers short-term pleasure but will cause cumulative damage to your body, which will be extremely painful and expensive.

Eat in-season food for freshness. Many health experts and chefs often say we should eat seasonally, or include foods in our diets that are grown at the same time of the year we eat them. The best consequence of eating seasonally is that we get the best tasting, healthiest food available, especially when the food is grown close to us so it does not spoil on the trip and is harvested at the peak of its season (although there is no real guarantee that it is picked at the peak of freshness). This means we are getting fruits and vegetables that have not had time to lose their flavour or their health benefits by sitting in a container for a trip across the ocean.

Here are a few things to keep in mind when you're hungry:

Water. This one works best for me. Staying hydrated is a great way to help reduce extreme hunger/cravings and help regulate the amount eaten to match needs more closely.

Yin-yang imbalance. According to traditional Chinese medicine, certain foods are more yin (expansive), while others are more yang (may lead to hunger). For example, eating a diet that's high in low-quality sugar (yin) may cause us to feel hungry even after eating. The body naturally craves variety in the diet to make sure it receives the full range of necessary nutrients. If you feel hungry, try changing your menu to see if you feel more satisfied.

Emotion with food. Being dissatisfied with a relationship, bored, stressed, uninspired by a job, or lacking a spiritual practice can cause emotional eating. Many people try to cope with uncomfortable emotions or difficult situations by seeking balance through food. Similarly, when we crave foods from our childhood, we may really be seeking the feeling of comfort those foods may have provided when we were younger. In this way, food is being used to fill areas that were not satisfied.

Nutrition. This is the only genuine form of hunger. It is the only hunger that tells us when our body needs more nutrients.

Clean home. Simply put, I can't eat junk if it is not there, so we cleared out the pantry and removed processed food from our home.

Surround yourself with healthy eaters. They say you are the average of the five people you spend most time with. I prefer to surround myself with people who make good food choices.

Watch less TV. TV time is associated with eating, and usually eating junk food. Instead, read a book, meditate, call a friend, etc.

Get enough sleep. Lack of sleep affects hunger hormones and neurotransmitters, and ultimately increases appetite and cravings, particularly for high-carb, high-fat junk food.

When it comes to our relationship with food, one of the biggest, yet most common, mistakes people make is focusing only on weight loss. That is why diet pills and liposuction exist. But almost without fail, people return to their normal habits and have nothing left to show for the torture they put their body through, except irreparable damage to their health and wellness.

Do you go Paleo? Ketogenic? Plant-based? How do you find the diet that won't only help you shed kilos, but will also improve your overall health? And how do you find the path that will lead to real, lasting change?

This is exactly where FeelGoodX comes in. FeelGoodX looks at the body as one integrated system in which everything is connected. Weight, for example, is not treated as an isolated issue, but as a symptom of an underlying health problem.

In short, FeelGoodX focuses on the following:
Keep it simple and stick to whole foods—that is, foods that occur in nature and don't require flashy packaging, like fresh fruits and vegetables, free-range meats, eggs, whole greens, nuts, and seeds.

Limit refined carbohydrates. I removed foods made with white sugar or white flour from my diet. This includes all standard desserts containing white sugar, as well as refined grains (like white rice) and foods containing white flour (like pastries and bread).

Every meal, aim to get protein, carbohydrates, and fat. This will create optimal blood sugar levels and stave off hunger. Some examples of great protein sources include grass-fed meat, free-range chicken, fish, and legumes. Good fat options are avocados, olive oils, nuts, and seeds. When reaching for complex carbs, try wholegrains like brown rice, buckwheat, and vegetables like sweet potatoes, Brussels sprouts, or artichokes.

Emphasise quality over quantity. Not all calories are equal. Whole foods fill me up and fuel me, whereas empty calories (like in candy and chips) only give me a quick boost but many times lead to a crash and hunger later.

Because our lives are stressful and we can't have everything that is good for the body, we must detox regularly, or at least twice a year. Consider starting with a 14- to 21-day detox program. Fourteen days is for those who have a generally good diet, and 21 days is for those who always eat processed food.

Detoxing is like preparing the soil in the garden before planting: we need to prepare the environment in the gut before sowing the seeds of wellness. If the gut is damaged, you can eat all good and healthy, but you won't benefit. The program is the journey of process to restoring your gut.

In just 14 to 21 days, you can not only lose weight, but also help prevent or even alleviate chronic health issues like Type 2 diabetes, joint pain, digestive problems, headaches, allergies, and acne.

While this program is intended for 14 to 21 days, I often modify beyond that so the detox is more sustainable for my coaching clients. This program takes a different approach to food: rather than focusing on how much you eat, it centres around *what* you eat—the quality of the food and the composition. One week before beginning, I suggest you start paying attention to your internal dialogue when it comes to food decisions. By paying close attention to food decisions, we are bringing those conversations to the forefront of our consciousness. That gives us the opportunity to make real improvements and then maintain and even build on those improvements.

It is important to notice what you are saying to yourself and how the little devil in you is trying to manipulate you. When you are able to slow down and see which of the hungers is driving your desire to eat, you can address them properly and make better decisions. For example, a dehydrated body may well ask for food instead of water because historically we have received so much of our water from food. So the next time you are feeling hungry, drink a big glass of water and see how you feel.

Most food decisions are really decisions to change the way you feel. With that in mind, slow down and pay attention to:

How you feel just before the desire to eat kicks in

How you feel just after you decide to eat something

How you feel with the first bite, and with all other bites

How you feel half an hour later

How you feel the next day

Even during detox, I suggest you avoid having the same meals all the time. I encourage you to seek out a variety of food sources and combinations. Many fail to get enough variety, particularly of plant-based foods. This might contribute to:

The build-up of toxins that are naturally and unnaturally present in those foods

A lack of certain vitamins, minerals, and other nutrients that may not be present in those foods

During the detox period, here's what to eliminate:

- All sugars and artificial sweeteners

- Alcohol

- Caffeine

- Gluten

- Grains, beans, dairy from cow's milk products

- Nightshades (tomatoes, aubergines, potatoes except sweet potatoes, goji berries, tobacco, peppers)

- Eggs, seeds and nuts (pumpkin, chia, peanuts, cashew nut, sunflowers)

- Fruits

- Oils (soy, grape seed, corn, peanut, sunflower, vegetable, canola)

What to eat and drink:

- Whole foods (nothing processed)

- Colourful non-starchy vegetables

- Good-quality protein (free-range, grass-fed, organic). If it is red meat, 50g each portion and limited to only 1-2 times a week)

- Healthy fats rich in omega-3 (coldwater fish, walnuts, flax seeds)

- Purified water, herbal tea, green and black tea, mineral water

- Small amounts of nuts that are not listed above

Tips for your 14- to 21-day detox program (as best as your budget and local availability allow):

- Look for organic, grass-fed, antibiotic- and hormone-free free-range poultry, eggs, and meats

- Look for small, wild, or sustainably raised, low-mercury, coldwater fish

- Choose organic eggs

- Look for raw nuts and seeds, and avoid those which are cooked in oil or fried

- Choose cold pressed and unrefined oils

- Peel your vegetables

If the word "detox" sounds too depressing, I suggest thinking of it as a harvesting season—a season of plenty marked by heavy rainfall, abundant hunting, and lush plant food options. When you think of harvesting season, you focus on high-quality vegetables, high-quality lean protein, and ample water.

This communicates to the body that "winter" is over, and that there is no further need for creating or maintaining stores of energy and fat. There is an excellent time for weight loss and body fat percentage adjustment.

I recommend you have two rules during "detox" or "harvesting season":

Rule 1   What you stop eating is more important than what you start eating

Rule 2   Every time you waver, every time you have a little voice in your head insisting, "But this is healthy food!", stop and return to Rule 1.

> *"Food has the power to heal us. It is the most potent tool we have to help prevent and treat many of our chronic diseases."*
> *—Dr. Mark Hyman*

WHAT TO AVOID & ENJOY

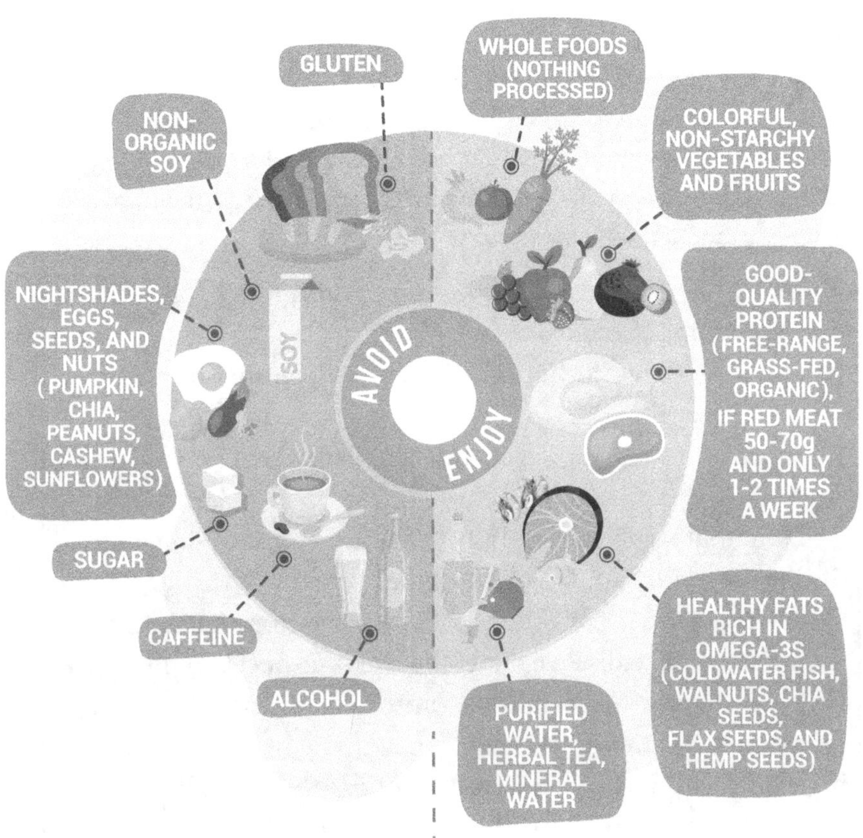

*Eventually eliminate all grains, all beans, and all dairy

*Eliminate fruits for this period and oils (soy, grape seed, corn, peanut)

*Small amount of nuts that are not listed in elimination

When you complete the program, if possible, reintroduce one item at a time from the "avoid" list to see how your body responds. And I strongly recommend you reintroduce sugar only in small quantities!

Sugar is like fire: a source of energy, but very dangerous. Our bodies recognise sugar as poisonous, and therefore rapidly activate multiple mechanics to reduce its concentration in our blood and tissues and trigger inflammation, which is linked to chronic illness like heart disease or diabetes. Sugar is also linked to neurological problems, including depression, anxiety, and autism.

Humans have evolved to handle only about 15g of sugar a day. Some tips to control sugar intake:
— Read the label to find out how many teaspoons of sugar are in one serving
— Check the serving size and calculate the percentage of sugar
— Note that sugar is high in fruit juice, soda, and sauces
Today, we eat over 68kg of sugar per year, or 500g per day.

There are more than 50 names for sugar. Food manufacturers realise we know the usual suspects, so they have become savvier. Supermarkets and health stores now carry many sneaky sources of sugar, disguised in unrecognisable ingredients and so-called "healthy foods" that actually contain as much as or more sugar than their regular versions.

"The food you eat can be either the safest and most powerful form of medicine or the slowest form of poison"
—Ann Wigmore

Sugar is prevalent in processed food today, and its effects on our brain chemistry are powerful. Breaking free of its grip can be enormously difficult. But as soon as you go through the FeelGoodX detox/harvesting program and take out sugar, you will see substantial metabolic and neurological benefits.

At the same time, giving up sugar can be challenging because our brains are programmed to love it. Sweet things from nature are always safe to eat, and they are quick sources of energy that have helped us store fat for times of scarcity. But sugar has become such a pervasive part of our food that we are overdosing on it.

Over the years, evolution has wired our brains to desire easy access to energy that the glucose from sugar provides. Our brains may be smart, but they still don't understand that all this sugar is killing us. In fact, eating sugar has an impact on the same parts of the brain that are stimulated by addictive drugs like cocaine or heroin. Many studies show sugar can be even more addictive than drugs.

The food pyramid below shows how much you should put on your plate.

The first pillar of the pyramid is water. Keeping hydrated is crucial for health and wellbeing, but many people do not consume enough fluids each day. Water has always been my drink of choice. It just makes me feel good. I tell everyone around me to drink water if they are hungry, achy, constipated, etc. Water is so beneficial, so easy, and so free, yet so overlooked. It is really a no-brainer (actually, our brain is 90% water!!!). Our body is about 60% water. The majority of our blood and every cell in our body is composed of water.

I don't get headaches and don't carry Panadol or Tylenol. I believe it's because I drink enough water. I have often been complimented on my clear skin—again thanks to my water intake.

FEELGOODX
FOOD PYRAMID

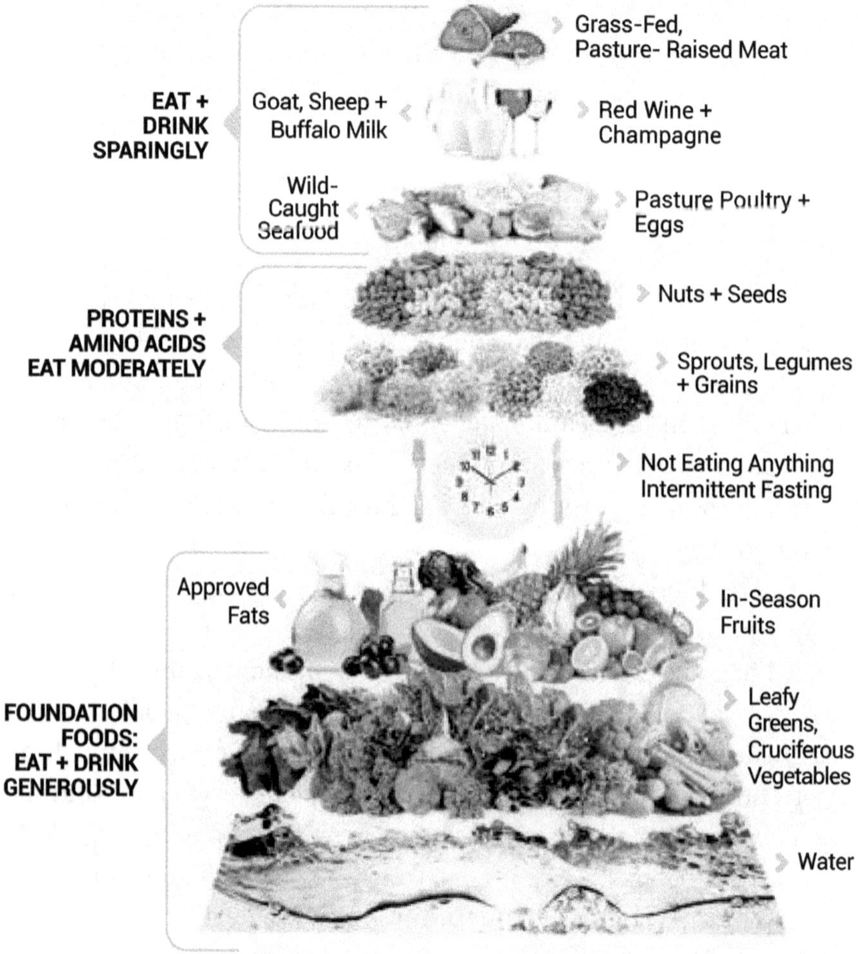

As with most things, the amount of water for each person is very individual. Some suggest drinking eight glasses a day, while others suggest taking body weight (in pounds), dividing it in half, and drinking that much in ounces. Listen to what your body needs. If your pee isn't mostly clear or you have any of the symptoms I mentioned above, you are likely not getting enough water. Foods with high water content, such as soups, tomatoes, and oranges, are also sources of water, but most of your intake will come through drinking water and other beverages.

Drinking water, whether from the tap, a filter, or a bottle, is the best source of fluids for the body.

Milk and homemade juices are also good sources of fluids, but beverages containing alcohol and caffeine, such as coffee and beer, are not ideal because they often contain empty calories. Drinking good water can help with weight loss, too.

The next section of the pyramid indicates the most important foods—the foods we should be eating most. Basically, I am in favour of plant-based foods. Plant-based foods are becoming a staple in many people's diets today.

There are a lot of vegetables and fruits in the market, but some are more popular than others. I educate myself on different vegetables and fruits to expand my horizons. Knowing how to prepare them properly helps too, especially if you think you don't like a particular vegetable. Changing the way you prepare it could change the taste completely.

Consider a large study from the Harvard School of Public Health. Over 200,000 health professionals without heart disease were followed for 25 years. A sample size this large and over so many years is uncommon, and it provides important insights into what we should be putting on our plates. That plant-based diets lower the risk of coronary heart disease (CHD) is not new, but this mega study helped cement this idea.

To take things one step further, I prefer the phrase "plant diet" over "plant-based" to make it clear that we should be eating *actual* plants, and not food made in factory plants. It is best to focus on plant-driven whole foods that are unrefined and minimally processed. This means pure, unadulterated ingredients that are in their original forms.

In fact, there are foods we allow ourselves to consume in unlimited supply. These include:

- Romaine, red & green leaf lettuce, mesclun (baby greens), spinach, endive, butter lettuce, parsley, fennel, seaweed, sea vegetables.

- Broccoli, cauliflower, Brussel sprouts, baby choy, cabbage, asparagus

- Avocado

- Extra virgin olive oil, avocado oil, walnut oil, sesame oil, coconut oil, rice bran oil. Fats are necessary for our cells, especially our brains, and can help lower our bad cholesterol and even shed weight. But the quality is important, and we should aim to get no more than 25% of caloric intake from fat.

- Eating fruit in season is a great thing, but as we can get fruit any day of the year, we have to be sure to consume in moderation, especially tropical fruits high in fructose. There are a few fruits that are great year-round, such as banana, mango, pineapple, and papaya, but they are better to eat while they are green. This is because they have not yet expanded their sugar content, and the good bacteria in our guts love to feast on these green fruits.

The next one is the idea of intermittent fasting. Our bodies actually need to go without food from time to time. From high-carb meals to eating the right kind of fat to abstaining from sugar, we hear a lot about what is best for our metabolism, but many new studies have found that it is not just what we eat, but also when. Intermittent fasting will help us not only lose fat, but also gain muscle and energy.

To understand why intermittent fasting works, we need to make the distinction between our body in a "fed" state and a "fasted" state. When our body is in a fed state, we are digesting and absorbing food. Generally speaking, we are in a fed state for three to five hours after eating. During this phase, our insulin levels are high and our body's energy is focused on digestion.

When our body is allowed to rest during the fasting, we experience a number of benefits. First, when we fast, we increase our levels of growth hormones as much as five times, which boosts our metabolic rate. Fasting can also reduce our insulin resistance, which lowers our blood sugar and makes stored body fat more accessible to burn. Some studies have shown that intermittent fasting may reduce LDL cholesterol (the bad one), which is a known risk factor when it comes to heart disease. Fasting may also provide a number of other significant benefits, including improved cognitive function, cancer prevention, and lower levels of inflammation.

There are many versions of intermittent fasting. I use the 16/8 method. This method revolves around a simple structure in which I restrict my daily eating period to eight hours. For example, each day I eat between 1pm and 9pm and fast for the other 16 hours. I do this once or twice a week.

The other days of the week, I go with a 12- to 14-hour fast. That would mean I can eat from 10am to 8 or 9pm, then fast the next 12-14 hours. So far, I find it is a simple thing that improves the functioning of my body. I feel really good when I do this regularly.

Sprouts, legumes, and grains, together with nuts and seeds, are okay to consume daily, but make sure to limit consumption of these foods to small portions per meal. And there are only certain kinds of nuts on the list—legumes, like peanuts and cashews, should be completely avoided. Instead, stick to the following:

macadamia nuts

walnuts

pistachios

pecans

chestnuts

Seafood, poultry, and eggs can also be eaten in moderation. For me, I focus only on wild-caught fish and organic eggs, but you can definitely include wild-caught seafood and pastured poultry.

Wild-caught seafood: fish is full of important nutrients like protein and vitamin D, and it is a wonderful way to get omega-3 fatty acids, which have numerous benefits like helping with various inflammatory health issues. It is not easy, but it is good to get wild-caught. Among other things, farm-raised fish are often injected with antibiotics, or even treated with pesticides.

Pastured poultry: it is not the same thing as free-range or organic. Often, free-range chickens are never shown the light of day, and they are fed with corn and soy. Pastured poultry is a sustainable agricultural technique that calls for the raising of laying chickens, meat chickens, and/or turkeys on pasture, as opposed to indoor confinements. It is also a more humane treatment.

Eggs: I love the scene in the movie *Rocky* when Sylvester Stallone breaks six whole raw eggs into a jar and drinks it in one go! Sadly, in the last decade or so, egg yolks have been criticised and condemned. Eggs are tasty as well as nutritious. Whole eggs contain about 6g of high-quality protein. Eggs are also a rich source of vitamins including A, E, and K, and a range of B vitamins, such as B12 (for energy) and folic acid. Eggs also contain all eight essential amino acids needed for optimal muscle recovery and for using valuable minerals like calcium, zinc and iron more efficiently.

Many people have asked me about the yolk! Eggs do contain cholesterol, but fortunately, dietary cholesterol does not raise blood cholesterol levels.

Dairy: Is dairy a friend or foe? The general answer is it depends on the individual. We are all different. For me, it is a no! I can't tolerate it, but I'm not sure if it is a casein intolerance or a lactose intolerance. Many studies have shown that consuming dairy is associated with a higher risk of developing multiple sclerosis and Parkinson's disease. For some, it can be harmful to health. Dairy is a common source of inflammation. If you can find forms of dairy that you can tolerate, great. It is nutrient-dense and ranges from delicious to divine. But if you feel bloated or you break out in eczema or acne any time you eat cheese, it is time to face the music. I have eliminated cow's milk from my diet, and instead stick with goat, sheep, and buffalo milk. I consider this an indulgence and consume only in moderate quantities.

Red wine and champagne: Red wine in moderation, meaning once or twice a week, can actually improve health. Red wine also contains resveratrol, a powerful anti-inflammatory antioxidant. Studies show resveratrol benefits brain health, helps balance blood sugar, and protects against cancer. An occasional glass can be one of life's pleasures that may also help your waistline. Too much can lead to a fatty liver, poor eating habits, nutrient deficiencies, weight-loss resistance, inflammation, and of course, a really nasty hangover. Because red wine comes loaded with antioxidants and other healthy ingredients, it is better than white wine, but an occasional white wine can also work.

If you love bubbly champagne, you can take one or two glasses a week. According to a 2013 study from Reading University, drinking one to two glasses of champagne a week could help prevent memory loss and protect the brain from diseases like Alzheimer's and dementia. This is said to be thanks to the Pinot Noir and Pinot Meunier grapes that are used in champagne; however, note that this study was conducted on animals, not people, so the results may not apply to a human model. And the study does not mention how the other ingredients in the sparkling wine, like sugar, could affect our health. So, consider saving it for a really special occasion. We can get polyphenols from other foods like blueberries and cocoa.

Grass-fed, pasture-raised meats are acceptable, but should be consumed only in limited quantities—my recommendation is not more than 115g a day.

Personally, I don't eat any meat for a few reasons, including climate change. Each meat eater is responsible for nearly 50% more greenhouse gas emissions than each plant-based eater, and for approximately 100% more emissions than for each vegan. That means that a meat eater has a carbon footprint about twice the size of a vegan's.

If you are concerned about environmental damage, health risks, economic problems, or ethical issues that plague the meat industry, you can take action immediately. Make a choice to buy less meat, fish, and eggs, or, better yet, give them up completely. It is one of the most powerful things you can do.

> **"When diet is wrong, medicine is of no use;**
> **when diet is correct, medicine is of no need."**
> **—Ayurvedic Proverb**

My classmate and Integrative Nutrition Health Coach, Kiko Hirakawa of kikosunflowersoul.com, suffered from a severe eating disorder that almost took her life. As a result of her work in the international modelling world, she began to develop a severe eating disorder, as well as other mental health issues such as depression, anxiety, and low self-esteem. She was always naturally skinny, but was told to lose about 5kg (10lbs). She felt extremely bad about being not "skinny" or "good" enough for the industry. When she went on an extreme diet with almost no knowledge of nutrition, her strict regime eventually led her to the emergency room. She was so weak that her doctors thought she was at risk of having a heart attack: her heart rate was 38bpm, and she weighed 45kg (99lbs) at 180cm (5'11) tall. She was so weak that she could easily fall over, and she was too cold to fall asleep.

Her key to full recovery was to learn to love herself. She started understanding that self-love meant more than just loving herself mentally. It also meant loving her body. She adopted a plant-based lifestyle built on vegetables, wholegrains, nuts, seeds, legumes and fruits, with few or no animal products. It was a sustainable solution for her health because when she went plant-based, she naturally cut out processed foods, unhealthy items like added sugar, and refined grains. Instead, she ate more whole foods that truly nourished her body and her mind.

At the same time, she also realised that true happiness comes from within. She learned to appreciate what she had and to not look outside of herself for validation.

Home Cooking

> *"You don't have to cook fancy or complicated masterpieces, just good food from fresh ingredients."*
> —*Julia Child*

My new habit is cooking. Cooking has improved my relationship with food and my body. It helps me to make healthy ingredients taste good or even delicious.

With cooking, I discovered that my body responded differently than it did to the outside food I had been eating. It gives me satisfaction and helps me feel energetic.

Cooking is a game-changer, but it took years for me to start. I had the same excuses as many do:

"I don't have time."

"I don't have enough space in the kitchen."

"Too many items to clean up."

Cooking is probably the thing that has had the biggest, most positive impact on my life. I began to find cooking rewarding, and that made me want to figure out how to make it happen day after day. With systems, preparing meals is easier and less of a burden. Once I started doing it, I found the confidence to make delicious food, and now find it easy to throw something together in a pinch from pretty much anything I have on hand.

I decided to make cooking a fun and creative process instead of a burden. The whole process, including clean-up, is only a mild to moderate effort, and the reward is real and tangible.

I often use a recipe or several recipes as a guide or template, but I am not a slave to recipes. If I want to swap out the recipes or protein type or add a sauce or put an egg on it, I know exactly what to do. From cooking with recipes to cooking without recipes, I developed my intuition and can make something from almost anything I have at home. When I am bored of a dish always tasting the same, as an intuitive cook, I know how to change it up just enough for it to feel fresh without having to reinvent the wheel.

If I don't really have time on weekdays, I can prepare in advance on free days. I plan my meals for a week ahead, and then, based on the plan, I prepare a shopping list on my phone, add to it as needed during the week, then set aside a few hours to make the meals and freeze them so they are ready when I need them.

At home, we also use a classic slow cooker to make soups, stews, and more. Without having to dedicate more than a few minutes to assembling the ingredients and hitting the "on" switch, dinner is served.

One of the latest and most fun kitchen gadgets we have bought is a spiraliser, a small device that slices veggies into long, spaghetti-like strands. Now, favourite meals are served hot or cold on spiralled courgette with homemade tree curry or raw *pad thai! Aroi Jing Jing* ("very delicious" in Thai)!

There are many health benefits to home-cooked meals. The most obvious is the benefit of controlling what types of ingredients go into your meals. When you eat out in most fast food, family-style, or casual restaurants, they are not focused on health, but on profits. For this reason, they use the cheapest ingredients possible. Unfortunately, this all comes at a high cost to our health since we are eating raw ingredients from large-scale industrial farms and feedlots where GMO crops, nutrient-depleted soil, pesticides, and antibiotics are the order of the day. Restaurant dishes may taste great and leave us begging for more, but don't let the seasoning fool you. Commercially prepared foods are infamously high in fat, sugar, and salt. They drown the food with sauce and salt because the only thing restaurants have to worry about is whether we will come back for more. When we eat out, we are not 100% in control of what goes on our plate. But when we make our own meals with fresh, local, or organic ingredients, each bite delivers loads of bioavailable, health-supporting nutrients.

Since cooking is a new habit, eating out has become the exception and not the rule for me and my wife. Occasionally, we'll still indulge at organic and farm-to-table-style restaurants, where more nutritionally dense, fresh, local, and organic dishes are served, but too much of a good thing can still hit wallets, so we make eating out a rare treat, rather than our default setting.

> **Real food doesn't have ingredients; real food IS ingredients.**
> **—Jamie Oliver**

I met John Tang, a young man in his 20s, in Singapore. He was kind enough to share his story with me:

I used to suffer from an arthritic-related autoimmune disorder for three years but through naturopathy, herbal medicine, nutritional, and lifestyle changes, am now almost "cured" and not relying on any medication.

I cook most of my meals because it is cheaper and much healthier than eating out. I get to control what goes into my body and have come to enjoy the cooking process. It gets my creative juices flowing as I try new recipes and flavours. It has become one of my favourite forms of relaxation after a long day at work or school. I've been preparing my own meals for the past six years or so, and here are some tips I've learnt along the way that I use to cook nutritious, delicious meals!

1. It's all about the veggies! When grocery shopping, I buy veggies according to the three types of vegetables we should all be eating that I learnt from following the Wahls Protocol in the past: a) dark green leafy vegetables, b) cruciferous vegetables like broccoli and cabbage, c) colourful vegetables like carrots and beetroot. According to the Potential Renal Acid Load (PRAL) of foods, we need to eat four to five times more alkalising foods like vegetables to balance the acidic nature of the proteins we eat and maintain an alkaline, anti-inflammatory, and disease-preventing state of health. So now you know how to portion your plate!

2. Batch cook! I do grocery shopping about once a week and soon after will cook almost everything I've bought in one shot. If I can't get organic produce, I first soak and wash in a diluted vinegar solution, then chop up and lightly steam (5-8 mins) anything that needs cooking, such as broccoli. Of course, raw is best, and I usually have a big salad, too. With that big pot of veggies, I either refrigerate them to use as ingredients for quick meals (see below), or I make a big pot of stir-fry or curry.

For protein, besides some eggs, I rarely buy animal products now. For beans and lentils, I soak them with water and some vinegar overnight, and then spice this up with some Mexican spices like chipotle and lots of paprika when I warm a portion just before eating. I also carry a small box of nuts and seeds to munch on every day.

I usually limit my carb intake to the end of the day or after exercising to stay lean. These range from steamed kumara (sweet potatoes) to rice noodles or porridge cooked in any leftover curry gravy for extra flavour! Sometimes, I roast a whole pumpkin and that's enough to last the week. Other times, I just finish the meal with fruits.

3. Quick meals! Because I've already pre-cooked everything, all I need to do is warm it up slightly (careful not to overcook!) and add some flavours (see below) before consuming. To save time, I prepare the next day's lunch while making dinner—basically just scooping what I need from the fridge into my glass lunchbox, flavouring it, and putting it back in the fridge. Next morning, this box is ready for me to "grab and go!" No heating is necessary, as the cold food will have warmed to room temperature by lunchtime.

Another quick go-to in case I run out of food or just feel bored of cooked foods is a salad. I buy the pre-washed ones to save time and add whatever I feel like adding—often some olive oil, vinegar, tahini, nuts, seeds, fruits, and seaweed.

4. Flavour and spice makes everything nice! These days, you can buy and experiment with many pre-mixed powder spices like curry, chipotle or Italian mixed herbs. For dinner, I usually do a quick stir-fry of onions, garlic, and ginger before throwing the refrigerated portions in and flavouring with a few teaspoons of those spices. I often add an extra tablespoon of turmeric and black pepper for their anti-inflammatory benefits. Other go-to sauces and flavourings are tamari (gluten-free soy sauce), nutritional yeast, pink Himalayan sea salt (salt makes everything nice!), preservative-free powdered vegetable stock, seaweed, cinnamon, coconut yogurt, and fermented vegetables like kimchi or sauerkraut! Mix and match, and keep experimenting! Every meal becomes an adventure.

5. The most cost-effective snacks! Think of the nutritional value of an apple compared to a bag of chips. Often, I can get a bag of five to seven organic apples for the same price as a bag of chips! An apple is not only five times cheaper, but it's sweet, and it really fills you up—it's often enough to replace a meal! I always carry a box of 'scroggin' (mixed nuts, seeds, and dried fruits) and some fruits in my bag. A banana is my preferred post-workout snack.

6. Trick your treats! Most nights I like to enjoy a nice treat after dinner, but many treats aren't exactly healthy or nutritious. The trick is to reframe your perception of what a treat is! These days, since going gluten-free, I like a nice treat of smashed avocado with flax seeds and various vinegars, spread on rice cakes. Other spreads include peanut butter, coconut yogurt, and miso with sprouts on top. An apple or orange can be a sweet and lovely alternative to some ice cream, too! Kombucha is an awesome alcohol alternative to finish the meal. Dark chocolate or homemade stove-popped popcorn is also nice.

Lastly, my recommendation for you is to have peace of mind. Stop looking for too many elements to work with. I am able to appreciate the beauty of food because I have experienced other genres of food as well. It's kind of like not being able to truly appreciate home until you leave it. It's okay to experiment with different styles of food, then return to plant-based food when you are ready. It won't be too late.

Because most ingredients are plant-based, the seasonality of ingredients is crucial. In terms of technique, preparing plant-based food is relatively simple; however, it is crucial that you understand the unique philosophy of appreciating the ingredients in order to cook it properly, wholeheartedly.

I especially love the key philosophy of Korean temple food: it is not about adding, but about subtracting. The taste of a dish should not be amplified by adding more things to it. The key is to use the bare minimum of good ingredients to maximise the integrity of the dish. Temple food requires only a handful of seasonings and sauces. That may sound like the food is tasteless or boring, but in fact, Balwoo Gongyang became the first Korean-style temple food restaurant in the world to receive a Michelin star in 2017.

How to eat healthy outside the home

I travel often and most of the time I find less-than-optimal food options. Sometimes I have to improvise and do the best with what I have. There are ways to plan so I can always eat healthily, even in the least ideal environments:

I carry healthy nuts, apples, avocados, and sometime a 70% raw organic chocolate bar.

I find the nearest grocery store to refill my healthy stocks.

I eat out smartly. I will research my options ahead of time and take note of a few ideal choices. I'll look for restaurants with healthy choices. Almost any restaurant can make a grilled/pan-fried fish or chicken dish with a large plate of vegetables steamed or sautéed.

A lot of my friends and family have told me that healthy food is too expensive. Actually, the amount of processed snack food that will fill you up is more expensive per gram than real, unprocessed food.

I eat only in-season vegetables, as it can completely change how we feel about vegetables and fruits. Happily, the in-season options also tend to be the best deals in the produce section. Leafy greens are some of the most nutritious, least expensive things you can buy. Frequently, half a bunch of greens with some beans, grains, and herbs is my entire dinner, and it costs around US$1.50. It also takes under 15 minutes to prepare.

Probably the easiest way to save money is to eat less meat. Whether from the grocery store or a restaurant, meat is always the most expensive thing on the menu, and *good* meat is even more ex-pen-sive! I do not advocate everyone go meatless like I have, but limiting meat to once or twice a week is an easy way to cut back on both calories and expenses. There's no need to worry about protein; just eat beans, eggs, and lentils instead.

Our tendencies may incline us towards cheap, greasy foods, but we should consider what we are really paying for in the long run. A poor diet can cause disease, diabetes, stroke, cancer, and a generally difficult, painful life. And I know that farm-fresh veggies cost less than a hospital trip and a lifetime of medication. Healthy eating does not have to be expensive, but unhealthy eating can cost you your life.

> **"Comes from a plant, eat it: was made in a plant, don't."**
> **—Michael Pollan**

The Japanese Okinawa diet has been in the spotlight for years, ever since Japan made a name for itself as the country with the longest life expectancy. Makoto Suzuki, a heart specialist from Ryukyus University in Okinawa, did several studies on the Okinawa diet beginning in the 1970s. Here's what he found out:

First, the Okinawa diet contains an incredible variety of plant-heavy foods with very small amounts of animal protein. In fact, locals eat up to 206 different foods on a regular basis, including a number of herbs and spices. For instance, every day, they eat five separate portions of fruits and vegetables. They like to determine that they are getting enough variety by ensuring their plates contain all the colours of the rainbow.

> **"Eat food, not too much, mostly plants."**
> **—Michael Pollan**

It could be thanks to its variety that the Okinawa diet is otherwise quite plain. The base of the diet is grains like rice or noodles, while seasonings like salt and sugar are used sparingly. In fact, Okinawans eat 60% less sugar and 50% less salt than other Japanese natives who already eat a diet that is relatively healthy by global standards.

Variety is important, but so are small portions. Okinawans say that you should stop eating when you are around 80% full. In other words, you should remain a little bit hungry. There's even a word for this concept in Japanese. It is called *hara hachi bu*, and simple ways to achieve it include avoiding dessert or reducing portion sizes. To practise the latter, Okinawans typically serve their food on small plates with portions of rice, vegetables, miso soup and a small snack, such as edamame beans. They instinctively know that eating less is good for them, and modern science has actually confirmed the benefits of calorie reduction.

By eating fewer calories, we can limit the level of a protein known as insulin-like growth factor. When too much of this protein exists in the body, cells age faster. As a result, eating less directly correlates to a longer life.

"Cheat days" are not a real thing!

Lastly, when I started my journey for better healthy eating plan I used to give myself permission to stray. That was what most people called cheat days! I believed that cheating was necessary to maintain a healthy lifestyle.

I realised this was wrong. Actually, it reflects a deeper belief that balanced eating is not enough. Cheating implies that eating a balanced diet is not 100% satisfying and involves sacrifices that somehow need to be made up for. It also implies that balanced living is an impossible task at which we can't succeed without sneaking around the system.

Admittedly, I may be biased as I really do love healthy food and am totally inspired and excited by all the things to do with vegetables and fruits. I get that not everybody is as health-crazy as I am. Having made one disclosure, here's a second: I really love (and eat) some unhealthy foods too, and I'd still consider myself a healthy eater or a balanced eater.

In fact, I would say eating *only* nutrient-dense foods is not balanced at all, especially if it means not letting myself eat foods that I truly love. Balance is a mix of healthy and unhealthy, nutrition and pleasure, function and fun.

It's a mix of eating nutritious foods I enjoy and not-so-nutritious foods I enjoy. We need both to be satisfied. There is no such thing as a cheat day. I can enjoy any food I want on any given day, as long as I own it, am aware about my choices, and am honest with myself about pros and cons.

Balanced eating is a fluid concept. It is different for everyone, and it's about doing what's best for our individual bodies. But like many things in life, balanced eating is easier said than done. We all have different emotional connections to food.

The good news, though, is that it is possible to change this. It just takes a lot of patience and practice to alter our mindsets. For me, it is a skill I build over time by staying open to possibility, testing my assumptions, and experimenting.

As mentioned earlier, I started a friendly dialogue with myself by asking these questions:

What do I really want?

How will doing (or not doing) this make me feel?

Can I change my thinking?

A little tip for you: it is important to consider both the present moment and the big picture when answering these questions, as sometimes, the responses are different depending on the context. Remember, having an honest dialogue with ourselves is where we really win. Balanced eating and living is not about a predetermined right or wrong; it is about making conscious choices with our best interests and true self-care in mind.

> *"Food is not just calories. It is information. It talks to your DNA and tells you what to do. The most powerful tool to change your health environment and entire world is your fork."*
> *—Dr. Mark Hyman*

Some other sources to inspire

If you're looking to take control of your health and adopt a better lifestyle, there are few better ways to learn than by watching a documentary. They're inspiring and usually well researched, and they take less than two hours to consume. I love recommending these to family and friends as a launching pad. If documentaries can do that for me, I'm hoping they can have a similar impact on you, too.

Forks Over Knives: Diabetes, obesity, heart disease, and cancer are all growing at an alarming rate because of our diets. Processed foods and excessive animal protein are why we are sick. These poor choices cost the world billions of dollars in medical bills. The solution is shockingly simple: eat a plant-based diet. Prevent and reverse disease. Take responsibility for your health.

Food Matters: We're poisoning ourselves with highly processed, nutrient-depleted foods. This movie brilliantly shows the connection between diet and sickness. We can't rely on pharmaceutical companies or magic bullets. Your health is directly controlled by what you put in your mouth. You can absolutely prevent, and even reverse, chronic disease by eating healthily.

Cowspiracy: As the title suggests, this movie addresses the global beef and dairy industry, and specifically what impact all these four-legged animals have on our planet. This film brings serious awareness to the sustainability crisis that we're not even aware of. Famous non-profit organisations are also exposed for not bringing this to our attention. You'll want to go vegan after this, but don't be scared by the challenge. *Cowspiracy* is an absolute must-watch.

Food, Inc.: One of the most famous on this list, and for good reason. Another absolutely game-changing documentary featuring all of the biggest names in the industry, including Michael Pollan. This 2008 film connects the dots between big business and government, farmers and consumers, convenience eating and sickness. *Food, Inc.* is confrontational, but also inspirational. We have the power, as consumers, to make better food choices.

Any time my diet is going off track, I rewatch one of these. My knowledge and determination goes through the roof, and I become the healthiest version of myself.

Healthy swaps

> *"The doctor of the future will no longer treat the human with drugs, but rather cure and prevent disease with nutrition."*
> *—Thomas Edison*

FROM processed and packaged foods and calorie-dense-nutrient-poor TO Mother Nature's nutrient-rich food

FROM refined, salt-heavy and unnaturally processed TO sea salt, Himalayan salt, and pink salts (loaded with beneficial minerals other than sodium)

FROM margarine (loaded with unhealthy, damaging fats) TO grass-fed butter (no damaging fats, plus nutrients such as CLA, vitamin K2, etc.)

FROM iceberg lettuce (nutritionally sparse) TO other lettuces such as romaine (5x lutein, 3x vitamin B5, 11x beta Carotene)

FROM artificial sweeteners (may alter metabolism and disrupt gut microbes) TO stevia (mainly positive effects demonstrated so far)

FROM chips and croutons (usually loaded with unhealthy oils) TO raw nuts (heart-healthy unsaturated fats with fibre and antioxidants)

FROM ketchup (loaded with sugar, fructose, and corn syrup) TO houmous (low-glycemic load and a good source of resistant starch)

FROM mayonnaise (usually loaded with unhealthy oil) TO low-fat plain Greek yogurt, olive oil, mustard, mashed avocado, pesto (basil + olive oil), and Mediterranean-inspired spreads

FROM cereals (added sugar and cheap refined grains) TO steel-cut oats or gluten-free rolled oats (dietary fibre and a whole host of cholesterol-lowering properties)

FROM fruit yogurt/frozen yogurt (added sugar) TO full-fat plain Greek yogurt with your own fruit mixed in

FROM industrial palm oil/grape seed oil, and canola oil (highly processed with a dangerous Omega-6-to-Omega-3 ratio of 700-1) TO coconut oil/rice bran oil, and red palm oil

FROM orange juice (a glass contains six tablespoons of sugar) TO a whole orange (full of water, no added sugar)

FROM dried fruit (easy to overconsume and has added sugar) TO fresh fruits (full of water, more difficult to overconsume, no added sugar)

FROM commercial salad dressings (extraordinarily unhealthy oils and sugar) TO extra virgin olive oil and vinegar (only healthy fats, no added sugar)

FROM egg whites (little protein) TO whole eggs (protein plus vitamins, minerals, carotenoids and healthy fats)

FROM wheat flour (rapidly digesting starch, nutrient-poor, often highly processed) TO coconut flour (high in healthy fats, fibre, and very low glycemic load)

FROM commercial bread crumbs (refined white flour, unhealthy fats) TO almond flour (full of healthy fats, vitamin E, protein and fibre)

FROM soy sauce (usually half wheat and half pesticide-laden soy) TO gluten-free organic tamari – no wheat, just fermented organic soy)

FROM commercial soups (loaded with preservatives and chemical flavour enhancers) TO bone broth (full of gut-healing proteins, minerals, and no junk)

FROM milk chocolate (low antioxidant value, more sugar, easy to overconsume) TO 70% and above dark chocolate (more magnesium and antioxidants, less sugar)

Hyperthyroidism

Gastritis

Dementia (together with a product called Cellec)

Fatty liver

Stomach ulcers

Bleeding piles

Constipation

Poor wound healing

Poor immunity in both children and adults, always falling sick

Cataracts and glaucoma and macular degeneration

Fatigue (this is one of the most common benefits reported)

Osteoporosis as PE regenerate collagen

Aging skin and hair loss due to inflammation.

Gotu kola

Pegaga is a popular ulam (traditional herbal salad) consumed by the Malays. In the west, pegaga is called by the common name Gotu kola. Gotu kola is used in recipes such as nasi kerabu, a traditional Malay rice dish, with herbs such as Gotu kola and turmeric leaf. Leaves are consumed either raw as in ulam and kerabu, or in juice extracted from the leaves. The juice is often taken with equal quantities of honey or coconut water. In the western herbal tradition, Gotu kola is well suited for people with a cold/depression or dry/ atrophy tissue state. Such a state may be characterised by dry skin (a sign of tissue degeneration), dry hair, slow metabolism, poor circulation, pale skin (due to decreased oxygenation of cells), and cold hands and feet. All are signs of aging.

The combination of increased breakdown of collagen, decreased synthesis of collagen, and poor metabolism results in premature aging of the skin and the aging process of the whole body such as degeneration of the joints and increased risk of atherosclerosis. The triterpene fraction of Gotu kola has demonstrated increased collagen synthesis and wound healing activity. This implies that Gotu kola is one of the most important remedies for delaying the aging process.

Numerous studies have indicated the potential of Gotu kola in neuroprotection such as prevention of amyloid plaque formation in Alzheimer's disease, dopamine neurotoxicity in Parkinson's disease, and mental ability in both adults and children.

The number of people with neurological diseases such as dementia and mental stress (food for thought: children and teens are mentally stressed out!) is steadily increasing in modern society. Gotu kola is a great remedy to relieve symptoms of stress, improve mental functioning, and reduce risks of degenerative brain functions.

Based on clinical studies and for best results, Gotu kola is best taken as an extract. In my clinic, we dispense a freeze-dried organic extract in synergy with other herbs to slow down aging of the skin and hair.

Red palm oil

Most people eat out often, and are thus constantly exposed to refined vegetable oils. Almost all food centres, fast food chains, and restaurants use refined vegetable oils in their cooking. Refined oils have gone through a series of high temperatures and chemicals to extract, bleach, and deodorise them. This is worsened by their repeated use in deep-frying, which generates lots of free radicals, which are associated with inflammation and cancer. Could this explain why we have high incidences of colon cancer in Singapore?

In addition, consuming refined oils depletes the body of antioxidants like vitamin E (especially tocotrienols). Vitamin E is a well established nutrient for healthy aging.

Vitamin E and A are very lacking in our food culture. Vitamin E deficiency is strongly associated with free radical damage, which is linked to many diseases like cancer, heart disease, diabetes, dementia, and allergies. Should you supplement with vitamin E? It depends on the types of vitamin E in your supplement. For now, consume a food that is high in vitamin E.

My observations tell me that the most important criteria for a healthy cooking oil are whether it is heat stable and whether it oxidises under high heat.

One of the best food sources for vitamin E and A is red palm oil. Red palm oil has a high smoking point and is heat stable. In addition, it is a very good source of vitamin A, which is why the oil is orange-red in colour. Vitamin A is necessary for good vision, which is critical given the amount of time we spend in front of our screens.

Alpha lipoic acid (ALA)

This is one of my most frequently prescribed supplements. It is naturally found in spinach, broccoli, potatoes, yams, carrots, and beets. ALA benefits the whole body, particularly the eyes, kidneys, pancreas, brain, liver, and the skin. Its main function is acting as a coenzyme for ATP production (cell energy). It is the only micronutrient antioxidant (besides the above herbs) that can boost the level of glutathione, the master antioxidant produced by your body that protects you from aging, diabetes, and cancer.

ALA detoxes your body of heavy metals such as iron, lead, copper, and mercury. It enhances cell efficiency, together with other micronutrients such as coenzyme Q10 and L-carnitine. This aspect is important for cancer prevention.

This is a must-have supplement to treat and prevent insulin resistance, the cause of many diseases, particularly heart disease, obesity, and diabetes. It is usually taken at a dose of 200 to 1800mg.

B vitamins

I supplement B vitamins in almost all my patients. This is because almost 80% of diseases I see are caused all or in part by stress. Vitamin C, magnesium, zinc, and all the B vitamins are essential for adrenal health and healthy stress response. I discovered their importance after I found out my eczema was significantly improved when I supplemented with B vitamins and minerals such as selenium, calcium, and magnesium.

As we age, our digestion and assimilation of nutrients decrease due to lack of stomach acid (beware for those who are on chronic antacid medications, which suppress stomach acid). Deficiency will increase stress hormones and inflammation, both factors that can lead to premature aging and fatigue.

The functions of the B vitamins are so connected that it is suggested to take a whole spectrum of different Bs rather than an individual B, unless under the supervision of a health professional. My prescription is normally a supplement of all the relevant B vitamins, such as B12 and B6, along with other minerals such as zinc, magnesium, vitamin D and selenium.

Fennel

The two most common symptoms of aging are poor digestion/lack of absorption and sarcopenia (loss of muscle mass). The latter is caused by poor absorption of nutrients such as calcium and vitamin D. Poor absorption is also caused by a lack of digestive enzymes. It is useful to supplement digestive enzymes; however, in my opinion, we don't want to keep taking it for something we are supposed to produce in our bodies.

One of the main herbs I supplement for my patients is fennel. Fennel is recommended as one of the best digestives and strengthening herbs in Asian traditional medicine. It stimulates the production of enzymes, improves liver and gallbladder functions, and clears the intestines of toxins and excessive mucus. Fennel also brightens the eyes, probably due to the presence of vitamin A.

Fennel is a probiotic—that is, it helps your gut to produce good bacteria. This is necessary for good immunity and a balanced mood.

Finally, fennel is a natural antidepressant that exerts a calming effect on the nerves and promotes mental alertness, without the similar stimulating effects of caffeine found in coffee and Chinese tea. It is, therefore, a suitably healthy supplement for stressed-out people. You can take it as a tea or supplement as a tablet.

Magnesium

In this modern and busy world of stress, magnesium stands out as the "anti-stress" mineral. In my clinical experience, I found many diseases are either directly caused by stress or worsened by it. High-stress hormones in response to constant stress are associated with many symptoms, such as heart attack, menstrual pain, kidney stones, fatigue, anxiety, insomnia, cramps, autoimmune diseases, arrhythmias, asthma, irregular periods, depression, obesity, hypertension, short-term memory loss, etc.

Magnesium deficiency is worsened by a refined diet and high-carbohydrate foods lacking in calcium, potassium, and phosphorus. Together with the B vitamins and certain relaxing herbs such as chamomile, magnesium is a crucial supplement to take to prevent stress-related disorders.

Many magnesium supplements cause digestive disturbances. One of the best forms of magnesium that does not have this side effect is magnesium bisglycinate chelate. It is most effective to take on an empty stomach and before bed.

Guidelines when buying supplements

The world of supplements is a complicated one for the average consumer. There are many technical details that we may not be aware of. We usually choose those that appear to be "famous," but this is no guarantee of the best. For example, many high-quality supplements used by doctors and natural health practitioners are not well known in the retail market. Nevertheless, here are some critical things you may want to look out for to make an informed choice:

Most manufacturers of supplements are required to adhere to at least GMP (good manufacturing practice). However, pharmaceutical-grade GMP is only legally required in countries such as Australia, Canada, Japan, and Germany. Pharmaceutical-grade GMP is also applied in some high-quality manufacturers in the United States. These products are usually used by qualified health professionals such as medical doctors, naturopathic physicians, and herbalists. Pharmaceutical GMP ensures the highest quality ingredients are produced with the same high standards applied to pharmaceutical drugs.

Third-party certifications

In the United States, an independent and accredited nongovernmental organisation, NSF, certifies supplements based on a rigorous process. If the product is manufactured in a facility with an NSF certification mark, it means the manufacturer's facility has been audited to comply with the FDA's GMP requirements. The formula and label claims have been verified. The label has been checked to qualify that what is on the label is what is in the product. Testing has been done to ensure there are no harmful levels of contaminants, such as heavy metals and pesticides. NSF scientists perform ongoing audits and testing to make sure manufacturers are adhering to certification codes.

Do some online research

Check for recalls, complaints, or very bad reviews; however, do not jump to conclusions just because of one bad remark.

Check any adulterants

Adulterants are defined as the intentional or unintentional presence of undeclared ingredients that have an adverse impact on the safety of the product. Intentional adulterants can be pharmaceutical drugs such as steroids to increase its potency or the substitution of one or more herbal ingredient with toxic species.

In addition, unintentional adulterants could be unsafe levels of heavy metals and other contaminants. This aspect is particularly a concern with raw herbs, commonly used in the Asian culture for soups and tonics.

Sometimes, due to the formulator's lack of professional knowledge and clinical experience, the herbs used may not be the right species for the intended effect. A cheaper alternative may be substituted for the actual herb. For example, the species of Tribulus (a herb for hormonal balance) in China is different from one used in Bulgaria.

How does the average consumer discern this aspect? These problems generally can be overcome by responsible manufacturer or supplier commitment to pharmaceutical GMP and third-party testing.

Supplier expertise and support

You can have all the tests and certifications, but at the end of the day is trust. We should look out for the supplier, the formulator, and the founder's background. Are they specialised in nutraceutical or herbal products? How trustworthy are they in the market? If they deal with herbs, are they herbalists who have years of clinical experience, or are they simply academic scientists? I have come across PhDs who formulated products that they have never used on themselves or on patients.

Are they users of their own products? If they deal with nutritional supplements, are they qualified and experienced in nutraceutical sciences and nutrition?

Many herbal formulations are made by non-practitioners who do not understand the synergy of herb combinations required for safe and effective consumption.

Last but not least, if you are not sure what supplements to take or what dosage, look for a company that provides professional coaching and after-sale support. Don't ask a sales promoter for medical advice. Seek professional guidance for your own health's sake.

FEELGOODX

LIVE YOUR LIFE, LOVE YOUR LIFE

Body and movement

Sleep is critical, and many of us (me included) are missing it in our modern lives. It is during sleep that lots of healing happens, and it's when our bodies detoxify while our brains process our days.

I once fell for the common myth that busy, productive people need less sleep, and that sleep is for lazy people. And for a long time, I would hack my system to survive on less sleep so I had more time. But not so long ago, I realised how wrong I was.

Most of us are getting far less sleep than we need, and a lack of sleep is affecting us in more ways than we think. If our body requires eight hours of sleep and we are forcing ourselves to get up after six and a half hours, we are skipping on 90 minutes of sleep every single day. This, according to one study, leads to a one-third reduction in our cognitive ability.

A study from Swiss psychologist K. Anders Ericsson proved that no one is born with innate skills. Being a great musician or artist, for example, is not about "gifts." It is simply about practice, but also about a second factor he observed in these great performers: they sleep a lot. Top performers sleep more than average people, getting approximately eight hours and 36 minutes of sleep each night.

And it is not just cognition. Lack of sleep has long been linked to obesity, but a new study suggests that late-night snacking may not be the primary culprit. The latest finding provided the most compelling evidence to date that disturbed sleep alters metabolism and boosts the body's ability to store fat.

The finding added to mounting scientific evidence that disrupted sleep influences the usual rhythms of the body clock, raising the risk of a wide range of health problems from heart disease to diabetes. Insufficient sleep appears to disrupt hormones that control appetite and the feeling of fullness, which ends up damaging the brain. The time of day when you feel the most sleepy might also make a difference in your health: aging adults who report feeling drowsy in the daytime, as compared to those without daytime fatigue, are three times more likely to have beta-amyloid deposits in their brains, a hallmark risk for future Alzheimer's disease.

Another new study from the European Society of Cardiology found that when it comes to heart health, six to eight hours a night is just right. Swinging below or above the number, though, may come with detrimental health effects. The meta-analysis is particularly impressive in that it looked at more than one million adults, all of whom were without cardiovascular disease in the five years prior to the study.

What the researchers found after 9.3 years was pretty stunning: subjects who slept less than six hours a night were found to have an 11% greater risk of dying from coronary artery disease or stroke, and those who slept more than eight hours had a 33% greater risk for the same events.

The author of this study, Dr. Fountas of the Onassis Cardiac Surgery Centre in Athens, Greece, made sure to mention that occasionally getting a poor night's rest or a day of sleeping in late isn't the major concern here; it is the prolonged effects that accumulate to create a problem. This study is especially interesting, as we have heard about the negative effect of too little sleep, but it is uncommon to hear that too much might be hurting us as well.

For me, a lack of sleep can also impact my mood. I am more likely to be moody and experience anxiety. It makes me think slower, learn slower, and solve problems slower. Not really a great state to be in.

I have made sleep a key part of my personal growth practice. Here is what I am doing:

I make sure I am setting myself up for success by being in bed for seven hours per night. It is best to work on going to bed and getting up at the same time every day without using an alarm clock. Test out your sleep by silencing that alarm and seeing how much you need for a few days.

In Bhutan, according to national surveys, around two-thirds of all Bhutanese people get at least eight hours of sleep per night. That is a lot better than most countries, especially industrialised ones. The effects of sleep on happiness, productivity, and overall health are extremely well documented.

Philip Gehman, PhD from the University of Pennsylvania Sleep Center, says, "Studies show that, over time, people who are getting six hours of sleep instead of seven or eight begin to feel adapted to that sleep deprivation. They have gotten used to it. But if you look at how they actually do on tests of mental alertness and performance, they continue to go downhill. So there is a point in sleep deprivation when we lose touch with how impaired we are."

Napping is my power booster! A 1995 NASA study found "a 26-minute nap improved performance 34% and alertness 54%."

Be active! Being physically and mentally active during the day can help us sleep better at night. In general, regular exercise improves sleep quality; however, some may find that intense exercise close to bedtime may have a negative effect on sleep.

Block blue light in the evening. Arguably one of the biggest factors disrupting circadian rhythms in today's society is our exposure to blue light, which is ubiquitous in the forms of fluorescent lightbulbs, mobile phones, tablets, computer monitors, TV screens, and more. Blue lights suppress melatonin production, delaying feelings of sleepiness and the onset of our nighttime cycle, disrupting, circadian rhythms and sleep. I don't bring any electric gadget into the bedroom and have no TV in the bedroom. The best strategy is not to indulge in any of these things for one to two hours before sleep; however, if you need to use your smartphone, use night shift mode, dim your lights, use amber-tinted light bulbs, and wear glasses that cut off blue lights.

Bright outdoor light in the morning. I find that sunlight exposure first thing in the morning has a substantial effect on my circadian clock and helps me feel more awake during the day. In fact, a lack of sunlight exposure may be more to blame for circadian disturbances than artificial blue light exposure at night.

Blackout and chill-out bedroom. I make the room as dark as possible at night and set the temperature between 16 and 19 degrees Celsius, which helps my body naturally cool and facilitates sleep.

I no longer drink coffee, but I shared with friends that drinking caffeine-containing beverages even eight to ten hours before bedtime can have disruptive effects on sleep. Thus, it is best to cut off caffeine more than six hours before bedtime. And while alcohol may help you fall asleep, it disrupts sleep quality. In other words, the more drink, the worse sleep.

I watch what I eat, and I don't go to bed too hungry or too full. I try not to eat within two to three hours of bedtime. If I need to eat something after that, a small, healthy snack, such as a handful of nuts, can be beneficial for weight management, appetite control, and body composition.

To recap, here's an easy 8-2-1 formula to encourage better sleep:

8 hours before bed, stop drinking caffeine. If eight hours is not good enough for you, go to ten hours. This is because caffeine is a strong stimulant, which can last well into the night before it finally wears off. When that happens, the quality of sleep is gone, which causes us to feel groggy the next day. So it is important to give our bodies enough time to rid themselves of caffeine.

2 hours before bed, stop eating. When we eat before bed, our body is forced to digest all of the nutrients in our food, which puts a dent in our energy reserves. Two hours will give our body the time it needs to digest our food the way nature intended and will let us wake up the next day feeling refreshed and full of life.

1 hour before bed, put all electronic devices away. That means no TV, mobile phones, laptops, etc. Personally, I love to read a good book before bed.

I am confident that the 8-2-1 formula can work for you, too!

Skin care

Many of us use lotions, sunscreens, etc. on our skin, perhaps even every day. Do you know what really goes in our beloved skincare products? When we put chemicals on our skin, it is actually way worse than if we were to digest them. Why? When we eat something, the enzymes in our saliva and stomach help break down the thing and flush out any toxins from the body. Unfortunately, personal care products and cosmetics absorb directly through pores. That is why people who use makeup on a daily basis can absorb almost 2.25 kg of toxic chemicals into their body each year.

I personally choose organic products over conventional ones to limit my exposure to chemicals that are potentially hazardous to my health and the planet. Let me disclose from the outset that I am a believer in the organic movement. I believe we have the power to harm ourselves or heal ourselves with our daily choices, and that choosing organic is one way to support our health and the health of the planet we share. Many people make organic food choices already, and the products we use on our skin should be next in line.

There is mounting evidence that ingredients like parabens, phthalates, and synthetic fragrances are causing myriad problems, from endocrine disruption to allergic reactions to chemical sensitivity. By choosing organic skincare, we are filtering out potential toxins and irritants in products we are using on our skin.

Based on reliable data that I found, here's the quick list of what to avoid and why:

- Parabens, triclosan and phthalates may cause endocrine disruption.

- Sulfates (especially sodium lauryl/laureth sulfate, or SLS) may cause skin irritation.

- Petrochemicals are known for pore clogging.

- Ethoxylated ingredients (anything that ends in 'eth', phenoxyethanol, polysorbates) may be carcinogenic.

- Synthetic colour is often derived from petroleum or coal tar, which has a possible link to behaviour issues.

Synthetic fragrance is highly allergenic and often contains petrochemicals and phthalates.

From my experience, I look for brands that seem authentic in their mission, transparent and educated in their communication, and willing to answer questions about sourcing and ingredients.

Everyone's skin is unique, and truly understanding your own skin is the way to go. It does not have to be complicated. Take stock of what you are using, and if you ever have an allergic or negative reaction to a product, see what ingredients are in it. Then, take a product that works well for you and see what ingredients are in that product. Over time, paying attention to ingredients helps you identify patterns, such as ingredients your skin dislikes and those it loves. Staying on top of your skincare game means understanding what works for you and understanding what your skin is craving each day. It can go such a long way toward helping your skin be at its best.

Years ago, when we visited Seoul, South Korea, my wife was impressed with the skin of Koreans and started asking those we met. From there, we looked more, and with that knowledge, I suggest applying the Korean beauty, or K-beauty, philosophy to your skincare. Koreans are masters at caring for their skin, and they are dedicated. Korean culture is sophisticated and conservative, with an emphasis on doing your best and being your best self.

At a young age, Koreans are taught proper techniques like exfoliating, moisturising, and using SPF, so it becomes second nature to them when they grow up. This is not just for girls; boys are equally invested in their skincare routine.

They even have products and routines specifically designed for those serving in the military. Personally, I totally ignored my skin during the time I did my military service in Thailand. For young Koreans, during their 20 months of mandatory service, men are exposed to harsh conditions, repetitive training, intense sun exposure, and extreme cold and dry weather. To combat the effects on their skin, they apply high-SPF sunscreens, wash their faces with foam cleansers, and hydrate their skin.

Koreans are focused on prevention and getting to the root of skin problems. They use products consistently rather than expecting immediate results from one use. This means applying SPF 30+ and moisturiser before fine lines and dark spots appear, not just covering them with makeup and hoping for the best. They believe that with time and effort, you can be in control of your skin. This long-term, gentle approach is what helps skin get that lit-from-within glow. This is the signature K-beauty, hydrated and bouncy.

Movement

Nature played a big part in how I got back to health after my illness. The sound of the forest, the scent of the trees, the sunlight playing through the leaves, the fresh, clean air— these things gave and give me a sense of comfort. They ease my stress and worry, and help me to relax and think more clearly. Being in nature can restore my mood, give me back my energy and vitality, and refresh and rejuvenate me.

In Japan, they have a practice called *forest bathing* or *shinrin-yoku*. Shinrin-yoku means taking in the forest through our senses—it bridges the gap between us and the natural world. Numerous studies have shown shinrin-yoku has real health benefits and that it will bring you into the present moment and de-stress and relax you.

So, how do I go about forest bathing?

First, I choose a park near where I live and leave my phone and camera behind. Together with my wife, we walk aimlessly and slowly. We don't need any devices. We let our bodies guide us. We listen to where they want to take us. We follow our noses and take our time. We are not going anywhere. We are savouring the sounds, smells, and sights of nature, and we are letting the forest in.

The key to unlocking the power of the forest is in the five senses. Let nature enter through our ears, nose, mouth, hands, and feet. There are many different activities we can do in the forest or park. Here are some of the things we see people doing: forest walking, yoga, eating, Tai Chi, Qigong, meditation, breathing exercises, plant observation. It does not matter how fit or unfit we are. Shinrin-yoku is suitable for any level of fitness.

Tai Chi

I started learning Tai Chi five years ago.

While many people are aware of yoga's powerful ability to heal as many as 40 medical conditions, most people are not aware of Tai Chi's incredible powers.

Tai Chi originated from the martial arts, and is today thought to improve mind-body coordination, breathing and movement control, and stress. Tai Chi originated in China over 2,000 years ago and uses continuous, circular, slow, flowing movements combined with breathing.

Tai Chi provides a wonderful way to connect with my whole body, come into harmony with myself, and learn to move more easily through all kinds of challenges. It also works to release stress, unblock energy where it is stuck, and heal everything from inflammation and chronic pain to digestive and immune disorders.

When I started, I struggled with the elements of Tai Chi:

- Softness

- Breathing

- Natural movement or a body practice

- Grace and coordination

Natural movement is our most efficient and effective way to move. It brings our whole self into harmony, with every part working happily with every other part. So why didn't it come naturally to me?

It had become unnatural for me to be natural because what I practised for much of my life was guided by a belief that if we are not suffering, we won't get anywhere good. Call it *no pain no gain*, or *no victory without battle*: this belief is an extremely self-limiting myth.

Guided by this myth, I disconnected from any feeling and intuition, isolated each part of my body from the others, and carried a great deal of excess stress and tension. This led to a loss of whole-self coordination and greatly increased the effort required to accomplish even simple things. It also made truly challenging things quite impossible.

We all have this potential to let stress go from our bodies and our minds. We all have this potential to do much more than we imagine, and Tai Chi can help.

Reiki

The word *reiki* means "mysterious atmosphere, miraculous sign." It comes from the Japanese words *rei* (universal) and *ki* (life energy). Reiki is a type of energy healing. Energy healing targets the energy fields around the body.

According to practitioners, energy can stagnate in the body where there has been physical injury or possibly emotional pain. In time, these energy blocks can cause illness.

Energy medicine aims to help the flow of energy and remove blocks in a similar way to acupuncture or acupressure. Improving the flow of energy around the body, say practitioners, can enable relaxation, reduce pain, speed healing, and reduce other symptoms of illness.

Reiki has been around for thousands of years. Its current form was first developed in 1922 by a Japanese Buddhist called Mikao Usui, who reportedly taught 2,000 people the reiki method during his lifetime. It is commonly referred to as palm healing or hands-on healing.

According to practitioners, the healing effects are mediated by channelling the universal energy known as *qi*, pronounced "chi." In India, this is known as *prana*. This is the same energy involved in Tai Chi exercise. It is the life force energy that some believe surrounds all of us.

This energy is said to permeate the body. Reiki experts point out that, while this energy is not measurable by modern scientific techniques, it can be felt by many who tune into it.

Reiki is alleged to aid relaxation, assist in the body's natural healing processes, and develop emotional, mental, and spiritual wellbeing. People who receive reiki describe it as "intensely relaxing."

Jean Michel Offe was a senior executive based in the corporate office of the same company that I worked for in Hong Kong. We have known each other since the early 2000s. He shared his experience with reiki:

"When you are dealing with cancer treatment, it is the body against the mind. Your body becomes weaker, but your mind must become stronger.

Reiki was unknown to me until a friend of mine suggested that I look at it to reduce the burning sensation on the skin of my neck enflamed by the cancer radiation treatment.

Initiating myself on YouTube on what reiki was all about, I decided to practise it on myself on a daily basis to appease the burning sensation.

After some research, I met a local lady who had practised reiki for the past 12 years. She came to my home to practise it on me and help me to understand it better.

After a few weeks, I felt mentally calm and physically strong, despite the constant pain on my throat.

I have now been in remission for over two years, and I continue my reiki two to three times a week, and even more if time allows it. I also enrolled in a course, and I am now level 3 reiki certified.

Reiki has had a lot of positive effects on me: I control my emotions better, and I have renewed energy, mentally and physically. I have combined reiki with the same discipline for my nutrition and physical exercise routine.

Reiki has also helped me to expand my mind when competing for the Hong Kong fencing team and in my sustainable coaching practice."

Thai massage

I can't leave this section on body without talking about Thai massage, especially since I see them all the time while I move around in Bangkok. There are so many Thai massage salons in Bangkok, and the number is increasing all the time. Traditional Thai massage has gained popularity in recent years due to its graceful yogic stretches and its ability to rejuvenate and manage various chronic conditions.

As massage modalities go, Thai massage can be one of the most peculiar forms of bodywork. For starters, it requires no creams or oils, and the recipient is fully clothed. Then, to make things even more strange, Thai massage is performed on a floor mat, with the therapist using their feet, knees, and elbows as massage tools. Instead of the relaxing gliding and kneading motions characteristic of more popular forms of massage, Thai massage employs stretching, pulling, and rocking techniques to relieve tension and enhance flexibility and range of motion. It is sometimes called the "lazy person's yoga."

The therapist uses their hands, knees, legs, and feet to move you into a series of yoga-like stretches and also applies deep muscle compression, joint mobilisation, and acupressure. Thai massage also utilises energy work, which, according to ancient Asian culture, treats the subtle energetic field within the body. It corrects blockages, deficiencies, and imbalances in the flow of this energy, which then is believed to improve the client's health.

Massage of all types is often used to relieve stress and protect against stress-related health issues. It is also said to boost energy and improve range of motion and flexibility. Thai massage, in particular, is said to ameliorate many different health problems. Specifically, it may:

Relieve tension headaches

Reduce types of back pain (typically subacute and chronic nonspecific back pain)

Relieve muscle pain and spasticity as well as joint stiffness and pain

Increase flexibility and range of motion

Stimulate circulation and lymphatic drainage

Boost energy

Calm the nervous system

A pretty common question is, "How often should I go?" Like everything else, there is no one-size-fits-all answer—it really depends on you, what your massage goals are, and the severity of your stress or condition. Remember that each person is unique, and the best idea is always to listen to the body. Try to consider how you feel before your massage, how you feel after, and how long your body holds onto that post-massage feeling. The amount of self-care you do at home will affect how quickly you recover. When working with an acute or chronic condition, it is important to wait until you consistently feel pain-free to drop the frequency of your massages.

Exercise

For me, exercise has become something that I love to do as often as possible, because it makes me feel good. This has not always been the case. I used to see exercise as a form of punishment for eating unhealthily, which never made the workout enjoyable. In truth, how many of us really enjoy being on a treadmill for longer than a few minutes?

After rebuilding my relationship toward movement and my body, I now use exercise as a reward because I know that when I do it, the results are tenfold. I feel good about myself, I have more energy, and I sleep better.

In addition, exercise helps many parts of the body:

Brain—exercise produces endorphins (the "feelgood" chemical), and reduces anxiety and depression. Exercise may also help increase recall ability and reduce the risk of Alzheimer's disease.

Lungs—exercise helps the body utilise oxygen and remove carbon dioxide more effectively. As the lung muscles strengthen, oxygen capacity increases.

Skeletal system—after age 30, bone loss can be inevitable, but continued exercise, particularly weight-bearing exercises, helps delay and slow this process.

Heart—regular exercise strengthens the cardiovascular system. The more efficient our heart becomes at this process, the harder and longer we can sustain physical activity. It helps raise good cholesterol and lower blood pressure. Being active may reduce the risk of cardiovascular disease by over 50%.

Digestive system—exercise is one of the best ways to reduce constipation and support regularity.

Muscles—exercising muscles helps increase our strength. As we strengthen our muscles, our lean body mass grows, which helps increase our resting metabolic rate, giving our metabolism a boost.

Skin—physical activity helps increase circulation and oxygenate cells, helping to keep skin healthy. Regular exercise provides an out for oxidative stress, which is a cause of early aging.

Ideally, I try to get in a 30-minute workout four to five times a week. Nothing amps up a workout and keeps boredom at bay like interval training. Since it does not require any special equipment, it is easy to incorporate into regular life.

Interval training is simply alternating intense exercise with less strenuous activity in the same workout. Depending on the length of the session, more intense activity may last just 30 seconds or several minutes. The pace and frequency of heavier exercise depends on individual fitness and endurance. At any level, though, switching things up results in greater benefits.

There are many reasons I like interval training:

It is good for my heart. Many studies have found that interval training does more for the elasticity of veins and arteries than aerobic exercise alone.

It continues to burn calories even after my workout is over. Adding bursts of more vigorous exercise burns more calories than continuous aerobics. Not only that, but calories also continue to burn off for up to two hours after interval training.

It results in the right kind of weight loss. According to a recent study in *The Journal of Obesity*, subjects who started interval training had significantly reduced visceral and abdominal fat after 12 weeks. Lean body mass increased along with aerobic capacity.

It increases stamina and aerobic capacity. Picking up the pace for just 60 seconds while jogging results in measurable improvement in blood pressure, and the whole body benefits from the extra fuel.

It improves maximum oxygen intake. Studies show that interval training increases VO2 max, which is the greatest amount of oxygen that an athlete can utilise during a tough workout.

It provides solid results in less time. When short periods of intense activity are introduced, moderate-intensity workouts need not be so long. Comparison studies between slow, steady cardio routines and interval training workouts have shown similar benefits.

When I'm really rushed for time, I go for Tabatas. They are short and incredibly effective. They only take four minutes to complete!

Tabata training is a style of interval training developed by Dr Izumi Tabata at the National Institute of Fitness and Sports in Tokyo, Japan.

How to do Tabata workouts? Go all out for 20 seconds, then rest for ten seconds. I will repeat this cycle eight times to complete the workout. I downloaded a Tabata app to my mobile and use it as an interval timer. I choose different combinations to cover different parts of the body. Tabatas leave me breathless, but they are worth every second.

Whatever program I do, I include different types of exercises that can help target specific parts of the body or are correlated with specific health benefits:

- Strength or resistance training to improve muscle and bone strength by increasing muscle tissue mass and the number of mitochondria that create energy in the body

- Flexibility to improve the range of motion of joints and muscles for enhanced natural movement, posture, and breathing

- Cardiovascular to improve blood circulation, which determines how well the body delivers and utilises oxygen and improving endurance and stamina

- Balance helps improve the body's ability to maintain equilibrium during daily activities

Get creative with your Tabatas. You can do them with any type of bodyweight exercise or traditional cardio activities. Just remember that to make them effective, you have to work as hard as you can!

I follow many experts and studies on quality over quantity. I do many of my routines super slowly, which I think is a neat trick. With other exercises, to make them more challenging, you usually have to increase the force required, which brings on aches and pains. This makes them more dangerous. By going super slowly, I can make exercise much more challenging without increasing force.

Running

This is the easiest sport in the world, and for many it fits into a very busy lifestyle because it can be done anywhere, any time. And it is free. It is one of the most straightforward ways to get exercise. Running is a great way to help improve cardiovascular health. Plus, it burns calories and can build strength, among other things. There is also a long list of psychological benefits that runners gain from running. At the beginning, it was hard for me—even brutal. But once my body and mind started to acclimate, running became blissful and meditative, and provided a sense of freedom.

The desire to run a marathon is still a mystery to me. But to others, it is the most natural thing in the world. I met Syahreelzal Kamaruddin, who is in his 30s and lives in Penang. His sport is running, and he runs all over the world. He has completed more than ten races since he started, including hiking to the peak of Mount Kinabalu, Sabah, Malaysia, in 2010, 2013, and 2017. Kinabalu is the highest peak in Borneo's Crocker Range and the highest mountain in the Malay archipelago, as well as the highest mountain in Malaysia. He has already lined up his plan to run 100 kilometres and a duathlon next year, and an Ironman in 2020. Here is his story:

"I started running in 2010. The first event I joined was Hikathon Penang Hill (trail run). It was in the "fun run" category, but was not fun for me! The route was the same as in the competitive category, except with fewer miles.

One of the reasons I run is for my parents: my father has diabetes and high blood pressure, and my mother has heart problems and high blood pressure. With a family history of illness, it would be easy for me to have the same symptoms. I have decided to control my food intake, go for runs, hike, and bike.

In running, there are a few categories: road running, trail running, ultramarathon road, and ultramarathon trail. The category I love most is road running. It's easy, I can run anywhere, any time, and it's free (if I'm not at an event). My opinion? Running makes me feel young, can reduce stress, and makes me look fit. Before running, my body weight was 78 kg; now it is 69 kg, which makes me feel confident. My body has a low metabolism, so putting on weight is easy for me. I try to push myself to run regularly. Even when it's a challenge for me, I try to run three times per week.

During long-distance running, you will learn how to control your emotions: when your legs and body get tired, the last thing left to keep you going is your brain and your mind. This will determine whether you stop or keep going. I believe running gives me mental and emotional strength.

Running also improves my energy levels. I feel tired when I've not run for a few days. Running makes me very active, regardless how busy and how stressed I am. It also improves my mood and helps me to stay focused on my daily routine at work.

As a Muslim, I run even during fasting, when most people will stop. On weekends I run in the morning, and on weekdays I run after 9pm. I feel even fresher when I finish my run during fasting.

Running also increases my confidence level. For example, on solo runs on the weekend, I always set my target to run extra miles. My longest solo run was 60 km, which took me from 6am to 4pm.

Having the correct type of running shoe is a big factor in preventing running injuries. These injuries can include plantar fasciitis, knee and shin splints, and Achilles tendonitis. A common treatment is to rest and apply ice packs to reduce pain, inflammation, and swelling. Using compression pants helps to avoid cramp and injury. Staying hydrated during running is very important.

Blisters when running are common, so a good pair of socks is very important. I always use blister-free socks for long-distance running.

Eating before running is a must. I prefer to have small portions heavy in carbs. Eat early so you will have lots of time to digest. I always drink coffee without sugar before my runs: aside from providing a performance-boosting caffeine jolt, coffee drinks are rich in antioxidants.

For full marathons and ultramarathons, I will bring oral rehydration salt, Himalaya salt, energy gels, energy bars, and dates (kurma). All of this gives me energy during running. Most event organisers will provide energy gels and bananas, but for ultramarathons, the water stations are limited and very spread out. For ultramarathons, some gear is a must, like headlamps, blinker lights, hydration bags or water bottles, a reflective vest, a mobile phone, and an emergency blanket.

Running speed depends on the individual. For myself, for half marathons and full marathons, my target time is under 2.30hrs and 5.30hrs, respectively. For ultramarathons, I prefer to run slowly, maintain my pace, and finish before the cut-off time.

Before entering a long-distance running event, the training part is very important. Gradually increase your mileage and pre-plan your training schedule. Before a marathon or ultramarathon event, I will make sure I run 30 km and above a week before, and I will rest for one or two days before the event.

Warm up and cool down before and after all runs to help prevent injuries. I also like slow and short runs (also known as recovery runs) the day after the event.

Your food intake is also very important: cut down on sugary, oily, and salty foods, and stop before you're full. If you fail to take care of your food intake, too much activity will destroy your body.

I believe all sport has risks, so don't overtrain, and listen to your body. Safety is your first priority. If you're running in the dark, ensure you use a light blinker, and wear a brightly coloured running T-shirt or safety strip to make sure people can see you. Always run against traffic."

Muay Thai (Thai boxing)

This martial art, with its roots in Thailand, has become extremely popular in many parts of the world these days. It is different from conventional western boxing and even kickboxing, as exponents of Muay Thai can make use of all four limbs. Learning Muay Thai has great benefits as it helps increase speed, agility, strength, and cardiovascular endurance. It builds up both stamina and overall health and fitness levels.

For generations, people have learnt this art not only for self-defence, but also for physical and mental wellbeing. It is a good art technique that induces fear in the minds of others, which is why scores of children and women are learning this invaluable Thai combat sport. For me, the benefit of Muay Thai is that it teaches me virtues such as compassion, patience, endurance, gratitude, and honesty.

However, a lot of my younger generation friends have now made Muay Thai even more popular, as it makes a person lose fat in the shortest possible time.

The most important factor is that the practice appeals to you, that you enjoy doing the movement on your own, and that you feel enlivened when you get done. Don't get discouraged if you find you are sometimes more aware of your physical pain and emotional pain like sadness, anger, or grief. That's part of the process of expanding your sense of yourself as alive in your own body. As you continue the practice, your pain tolerance will increase, and your felt pain will decrease and fold into a clearer, happier, more complete, and more functional you.

There is no excuse for not staying fit and healthy while we travel. There are a lot of ways to exercise without equipment, and also there are so many streaming videos on-demand and in-app that keep us connected to our fitness coaches and workout buddies. There are also many fitness videos that are specifically designed for use in a hotel room.

Exercise is a no-brainer. Exercise is not just good; it is great for basically everything! Unfortunately, many people assume exercise is solely a tool for weight loss, and while it does effectively help with weight management, exercise also improves mood, protects against a list of chronic diseases, and improves quality of life, to name just a few benefits. If you are not already exercising daily, do not worry about how much—just get moving. Start by committing at least ten minutes a day; you can even split up your exercise sessions. Every bit counts!

FEELGOODX

LIVE YOUR LIFE, LOVE YOUR LIFE

Finances

> *"Money isn't everything, but it is right up there with oxygen."*
> *—Zig Ziglar*

Ultimately, money is energy. It is important to know what to do with it. For me, it is about being able to have experiences in this world and share them with my friends and family, and it is certainly about security.

I don't have a proper financial education, but I am interested in where my money is going, so transitioning to a mindset of ownership and excitement has been an important shift. When I am excited about my own financial health, I can do something about it. If I don't look at it, I am not going to get very far.

> *"When I was young, I thought that money was the most important thing in life. Now that I am old, I know that it is."*
> *—Oscar Wilde*

When I was young, money was like sand slipping through my hands. It did not feel particularly useful except to fulfil some of my needs or dreams. Back then, if I'd had more tools, I would not have been looking for gratification through clothes or those types of external things. I realised that there was nothing I could buy to "fix" me. Then, I got to the point when I realised that stuff does not really matter. I wanted more purpose, depth, and connection to what I was doing.

I wish I had been more interested in saving and investing during that time of my life. It does not take a lot. If I had spent US$200 on good foundation stocks like Apple or Amazon, it would be worth many times that by now. Back then, I did not think that way, but I wish I had.

I think money is the single biggest problem I have because this is a subject that we don't learn in school. It was only by making ton of mistakes that I slowly came up with system that transformed my situation. It is a comprehensive system with structure and techniques to fix my financial life, for life. This is not a fast track but a system to wealth over a lifetime. Over time, my effort pays off.

I don't want to look rich and be living paycheque to paycheque anymore. Actually, we are trying to look a certain way for people who don't even care, and about whom we don't even care.

I want to be in a position where I have control and don't feel like I am constantly thinking about or working toward money—a position where I can move from point A to point B without a lot of stress.

The idea is all about how money flows in my life. In the past, I didn't know where the money went. I knew I was making money and then, all of a sudden, I got to the end of the money and there was nothing left, or I would get to the end of the year and it was gone. Well, that is the whole key to money: I needed to know where it was going.

There are two books that really changed me for the better: *Think and Grow Rich* by Napoleon Hill and *The Richest Man in Babylon* by George Samuel Clason. Both are books that many have recommended as must-reads in our lifetime. *The Richest Man in Babylon* is like the bible of financial freedom.

After having read both books, I now do something very magical with each dollar I earn. It's called paying myself first. Paying myself first means when I earn a dollar, the first person who gets paid is me! That means that money goes directly into a "pay myself" account.

> **"Do not save what is left after spending, but spend what is left after saving."**
> **—Warren Buffett**

> **"Save your money. You are going to need twice as much money in your old ages as you think."**
> **—Michael Caine**

Whatever that account is, the key to paying yourself first is that money moves right from your paycheque directly into your "pay myself" account. It has been nearly a century since this idea was first coined by Clason, an American entrepreneur, and it is still solid advice. Paying yourself first means that before spending any income, we must put some of it away. It is best to automate the process, diverting funds into a separate account so they seem less available. We can't spend the cash that is out of sight, the logic goes, or miss the money we never "had" in the first place.

The average person is saving somewhere between 3-5%, but I save between 10-15% (before taxes). Everybody should start saving at least 5%, but if you think there is no way you could start with 5%, start as low as 1% a month; just start. Saving money is like exercise. If I want to run a marathon, I am not getting up and going in tomorrow, no matter how motivated I am. We can't run a marathon from scratch. It is not happening. But we have to start somewhere. So the first step is to pay myself first.

From there, I build an emergency account. I was recommended to have three months' worth of expenses in the account. I, however, go for six months. I think six to 12 months of expenses is better. More is, of course, better. My emergency money is not sitting in the same account as the one I access with my ATM card. I set up a separate savings account. The key to emergency account money is that it has no ATM card, but I can still access it online. I put 5% of my money into this account. This is handy as I feel secure if I get sick, I lose my job, or my old car stops running.

The next account that I set up is a FeelGoodX account. It is an account that is about guilt-free spending. It is a place to pile up cash with the intention to spread it, guilt-free, so I can create memories today that I will never have if I don't. New experiences, new memories, new gadgets—whatever it is that helps me live the life I love today. This is where I save up for my holidays, things that I want to buy, learning subscriptions, or courses that will improve my skills. I make a point to travel with my wife at least once a year to somewhere I love or have yet to visit. Many people avoid this because it seems so expensive. It's not necessarily more expensive, but more than just robbing yourself of memories, you are sabotaging your productivity. A spirited vacation will leave you feeling rejuvenated, ready to work faster and harder than ever before. It is like when I have a good night's rest and start again in the morning, rather than working until late at night. Recently, I used this account to take two years off. Taking a sabbatical was the most important thing I have ever done in my entire life. I would not be writing about FeelGoodX if I had not taken a sabbatical. Deposit money into this account in proportion into how fast you want your dream to be funded—anywhere between 1-10%.

Apart from the "pay myself" account, which is before taxes, the rest of these accounts are contributed to after taxes.

The next category is credit cards and bills. Years ago, I was not smart and paid only the minimum on credit cards. I learnt that by making minimum payments, the average time it would take to pay them off was 27 years. It is the biggest scam in the history of humankind, financially speaking. Now, I make full payments.

The next place my money goes is toward automatically paying my regular bills. My regular bills are car, phone, utilities, and mortgage. Every month, I go through every single bill to understand which payables are subtracted automatically from my paycheque. I could go on the road for a month, and all I'd really have to do is check in and make sure nothing had gotten missed because 95% of my financial life is automatic. I would say that even my business is 80% automated at this point. This is because there are always things that come up in business that you can't automate.

The next one on the list is charity. The common theme among high-net-worth individuals (that is, people who have a net worth of over $20 million) is that they started giving back before they were wealthy. It is a fulfilling act when I know I have given to somewhere worthwhile to me.

Just to recap:

- Pay myself first
- Have the money moved automatically to separate accounts
- Automatically pay credit cards and bills
- Give to charity

Finding the money

I mentioned earlier that I didn't always know where all my money went. I would say things like, "You know, I make all this money, I don't know where it goes. It just goes. Like water!" Well, it goes in lots of directions. If we don't have a plan for it, somebody else does.

When I worked in a corporate office, many of my colleagues would buy coffees, lattes, croissants, muffins, and buns on the way to work. Let us do some maths now: say that morning run costs $5 before you've got to work. During the break, juice and snacks may cost another $5. $10 a day is $300 per month. That is $3,600 per year. If this $10 a day went into an investment instead, it would result in a totally different financial situation. The whole thing is life-changing.

I make my morning drinks at home for 20 cents. We need to look at where money is going in our life. Everyone is different!

For most, life without coffee is not an option, and brewing your own at home can be tough when you are already late and trying to get out of the door with your hair brushed and clothes on. In this case, I suggest feeding your bean need for less:

- Sign up to be a reward member to get benefits

- Order a short espresso. It gives the same amount of caffeine as a tall coffee for less.

- Go with brewed coffee instead of a latte, and it will be half the price.

- Order a double espresso over ice, then add your own milk and (if necessary) sugar over at the bar counter. You just made a cheap latte!

Track your expenses for 30 days. If this is too difficult, do it for seven days or even for a day. The key to this is: don't change who you are, don't change how you behave. Just be who you are always. Be your normal self, and spend money the way you normally spend it. This is a way to track where you spend money every day.

Another thing I did was go through my fixed expenses. Was there anything that I was spending money on that I didn't need or could get for less?

I could manage to change my cable package, my mobile phones, and my gym. I asked myself how I could get the same thing for less money. From there, I looked at eating out and entertainment. With this, I could save 10% and it changed my financial situation. This is where the money comes from to pay off debt. Having gone through all my expenses manually and looked at what I could renegotiate, I started saving, and my dream account grew bigger and faster.

My wife and I regularly discuss our finances, and not only during bills or tax payment time. We talk about how to get finances organised, what our values are, etc. We work on just one thing at a time. For example, a small purchase could cause issues in a relationship if you are not on the same page about what counts as "small." With clear communication, we create trust and honesty.

Paying myself first

I have tried budgeting, but it did not work because budgeting does not stick. We fight about budgets and go off budgets. Budgeting is harder than even dieting and, as mentioned earlier, I don't think that dieting works either. It is not a sustainable lifestyle. The sustainable plan when it comes to my money is to pay myself first. It has become a philosophy in which I believe the first person who should get paid from my paycheque is me! Like lots of people, I got this wrong. I believed that disposable income minus consumption equalled savings. Unfortunately, it is disastrous for me (and most middle-class people). It means we usually spend everything we make and have nothing left over to save. It is impossible to build wealth when you are in this wrong system. I found that wealthy people practise the opposite. They believe that income minus savings equals disposable consumption. Big difference. They make this equation the first step to building their own wealth.

In this way, we mentally establish saving as a priority. We tell ourselves that we are our most valuable asset. This is moving from the traditional way of spending money in this order: 1) bills, 2) fun, 3) saving. When we set the money aside before anything else, we adopt the mindset of the wealthy. If we want to be wealthy, we have to do what the wealthy do.

In the real world, when we earn a dollar, who gets paid first? The government! And on average, they take about 15-30%, in addition to other taxes that we have to pay. We are losing a quarter of our paycheque to taxes and, again, it is taken from us automatically.

I thought about my money on a clock face. When I worked for a corporation, I started at 9am. The first 2.5 hours of my day went to taxes. Then, I worked from 11:30am to lunchtime for my mortgage. It is very common that a full third of our paycheque goes to housing. Then, I got transportation costs. My car, insurance, petrol, or even public transportation, costs at least an hour of work. Then, from 3pm to 6pm, I worked for everything else, like food, healthcare, credit cards, entertainment, and all the other stuff I do in my life.

The idea behind budgeting is that I would somehow come up with a way to, at the end of the day, have a little sliver of money left over to save, but it never worked! I always got to the end of the paycheque and the end of the year with no money. This approach to wealth does not work. What works is to pay myself first, during hour one.

For nine working hours a day, the percentage is 11.1%. That was my starting point—that was what I paid myself before reaching 15%. I save an hour a day of my income to build financial security for life. On average, I worked more than 2,500 hours a year. The question I asked myself was: if I am going to trade all that time for money, shouldn't I be the first person to get paid? If I can't save at least an hour a day of my income, something had to change.

From the Fidelity study in the USA, I can recap as follows:

- People are continuing to save

- Three out of ten savers increased their contribution rate througout 2017. The average contribution rate is now 8.6%. This is the highest percentage in almost ten years, not including employer contributions

- Fidelity's suggested total saving rate of at least 15%, including employer contributions, is a marathon, not a sprint

FEELGOODX
WAYS TO ACHIEVE FINANCIAL INDEPENDENCE

01 VALUES

What we believe in

02 GOALS

What is our "why" and what are our targets in life

03 PAY MYSELF

Account that we save for later in life

04 EMERGENCY

Saving for urgent needs like job loss or special care for family members

05 FEELGOODX

Short-term to guilt-free spending on anything you want to do

AFTER TAXES

06 GIVING

Sharing with the less fortunate and donating

07 EVERYTHING ELSE

Monthly spending like rent, bills, food, necessities

Debts

With all those payments going out each month, there was nothing left for me. To get out of debt, I changed my habits, created margin, earned more income, and began to eat healthily. This is how I did it:

I listed all debts in order from smallest total balance to largest. If the debts had similar balances, I paid off the one with the highest interest rate first.

I paid as much as I could on the card with the smallest balance. I made only minimum payments on all other debts and put everything I could into the first debt. This motivated me to see them crossed out one by one. It made me feel good to see, "Oh, okay, I can do this." There are plenty of free calculators that you can use. I went **to find an app**, plugged the number in, and learned how long it would take to pay this debt off.

Another important factor is not to put off saving to pay off debt. We need to do both. If I have $1,000 a month, I put $500 for debt and $500 for savings. I disagree with the idea of paying off all the debts first. It is too depressing because progress can't be seen, and there is no saving.

Seeing my net worth go up and debt go down kept me moving forward.

The worst thing about credit cards is the high interest rate, but sometimes we can get lower rates. As a good credit card customer who pays on time, you may be eligible for a lower rate. If your rate is lower, getting out of debt is much easier and much faster.

Lastly, I live with the mantra that I don't spend what I don't have. I don't put things on credit. If I don't have it in my bank account, I am not charging it.

Financial protection

The emergency account is my money airbag. I started building up slowly to reach six months and now have 24 months of expenses saved. Bank interest rates are pretty low, typically less than 1%, so I have placed this money in money market accounts, time deposits, and savings bonds. These are great places to put emergency money. The whole key to emergency money, again, is that it is only for emergency purposes. I regularly check around and compare rates through various websites. The difference between a bank account and the highest paying money market account can be up to 100 times in the case of the difference between 0-1%. If I have this much money and I switch it to money markets, how much more is it a year? Big difference. When I choose money market accounts, I only look at those from recognised financial service companies.

I have a will, but am not a big believer in life insurance apart from that to protect your family in case you die early. If you have dependants and debt, and you want a protection plan for your family, you can go out and buy level term life insurance. Typically, it should be 20 years or more. People normally buy it when they have kids and they want to make sure that if something happens to them and they die early, their kids and spouse are protected. Life insurance is not expensive, especially if you buy it when you are young and healthy. It may cost less than ten cups of coffee a month. Just think: it costs less than ten cups of coffee a month to protect your family.

Build a FeelGoodX account

Anything you want to do between now and retirement is saved for in this account. This includes holiday plans, buying a home, and learning new skills. I made my own mind map to see my **FeelGoodX.** As a couple, my wife and I brainstorm and write out of all **our wishes**. Then, we go through what we are really excited about and look at the cost. Often, many of our **wishes** don't require money, just action. Getting our dreams down on paper can show us things we haven't yet talked about. Like the "pay myself" account, I create investment accounts that match the time horizon for my dreams. If the time horizon is short, like less than two years, I save the money in a money market account; if it is two to five years away, I look at bond funds. Beyond that, I check out stock funds or even blue-chip stocks.

Lastly, this transforms the journey to financial freedom into a system, and that is the secret of the ultra-wealthy. They create systems to simplify all their finances. With a system in place, you can make complicated financial decisions very quickly, without all the stress most people put themselves through. It will make your life easier. Basically, a system is a process for getting something done, and I use mental frameworks that help me make decisions rationally and logically. In many cases, I just pose questions that can be answered "yes" or "no", and then count up the answers. Decision made and stress removed. Your journey can start from your commitment with an open mind to making it happen. Everything changes when you make the mental shift to focus on cash flow. Then, you don't have to wait long to enjoy life. You don't have to sacrifice or delay your FeelGoodX to the future if you are meeting your financial objectives today. This is not a bet that you have to worry about whether you've made the right choice years down the road.

Be a homeowner, not a renter

Owning your own home is a common dream. There is no doubt that having your own address comes with a lot of satisfaction and pride; it also comes with plenty of extra costs and maintenance.

I have found the checklist at daveramsey.com to be very helpful, and can recap it as follows:

- Are you ready to buy?

- Are you out of debt?

- Have you built up an emergency fund with three to six months of expenses saved?

- Do you have enough cash for a 10-20% down payment on a 15-year, fixed-rate mortgage?

- Will your mortgage payment be 25% or less of your monthly take-home income?

- Do you plan to stay in the same location for more than three years?

You must answer "yes" to all these questions before purchasing a home. If not, it may not be the right time.

With real estate, it is better to buy the right thing at the right time. Only buy when you are financially ready.

Advantages and disadvantages of buying a house:

Advantages

- Every payment brings you closer to owning the house

- You can cash in on the appreciation of your house's value

- You have tax advantages

- You have the freedom to renovate your house

- !t is yours

Disadvantages

- It is more difficult to travel and relocate

- You have more expenses

- You are responsible for the upkeep of your home

Learning must never end!

> **"Live as if you were to die tomorrow. Learn as if you were to live forever."**
> **—Mahatma Gandhi**

I always allocate money for ongoing learning. Life is a never-ending learning process. Learning in life should not be limited to our school years. It should extend far beyond that, as learning is a beautiful, enriching experience that widens the horizons of your mind and enhances your thinking capabilities.

My thinking is that one must always keep the path open to new experiences. Always be willing to learn new things, discover the unfamiliar, and venture into terrains that previously looked difficult or challenging. Set new goals and objectives. Enlightenment is essential for gaining new experiences in life. These experiences will help us become better people and help us deal with the challenges life throws at us.

There are always new things to learn and discover: study new languages, cultures, norms, societal values, locations, and history. Find out why squirrels bury nuts and octopuses have three hearts. Keep learning new things every day; it will keep you fresh and energised and keep your brain cells active. The world is a big whirlpool of knowledge. There will always be stuff we don't know and facts we were not aware of.

I love reading. Reading has always been a fundamental part of the learning process. Reading increases your knowledge and makes you wiser. A good book can teach you what many other mediums may not.

> *"Books make great gifts because they have whole worlds inside of them." —Neil Gaiman*

Books include a large amount of information, which is the reason they have always been treasured by the wise. There is no better pastime than reading a good book, nor a greater friend.

Holidays are a good time to spend learning new stuff. Found something that has intrigued you, but have never had the time to explore it? Plan to research it during holidays. List the important points. Make a journal. Also, exchange with friends what you learned over the summer, and schedule an intellectual conversation over topics of interest. Share what you've discovered. Learn new skills. A friend knows a special skill? Show some eagerness, and request that friend teach you too. Someone knows how to fix everyday household items? Ask them to show you how to do it.

Learn glass painting, origami, cooking, website designing. Anything—just don't limit yourself.

We are lucky to have the web at our disposal. Tutorials ranging from cooking classes to how to learn anything can be found online. Make good use of it, and increase your productivity by learning new skills and trying your aptitude at a talent you might not know existed in you. Trying new things is also very good therapy to relieve stress from everyday chores. Make it part of your routine to try new things, and bring your friends along too.

There is no age barrier in the learning process. Being a student is one of the best feelings. Be a student again!

I save money for online courses, seminars, and books. I recently joined an online course to learn speed reading! I read about 20 books a year—nothing compared to many others like Bill Gates, who reads 50 books per year. A host of successful people know that reading is essential for learning new things, thinking differently, and becoming wiser day by day. This, in turn, means they can make better decisions in their life and work, and it paves the way to a successful life. Elon Musk has said that he learned how to build rockets by reading books.

> *"Books allow you to fully explore a topic and immerse yourself in a deeper way than most media today."*
> *—Mark Zuckerberg*

Buying a car

The ads everywhere say, "New Car! New Car!" A brand new car looks and smells good, but it's never worth the price. Nothing I do in my lifetime could waste more money than buying a new car. It's probably one of the worst financial decisions I could make. It is hard on the wallet.

Why? Because the moment we drive it off the lot, a new vehicle starts to depreciate: our car's value typically decreases 20-30% by the end of the first year, and in five years it can lose 60% or more of its initial value.

To make matters worse, like most people, I borrowed money to buy that car. Why would I borrow money to buy an asset that immediately goes down in value by 30%?

The good news is we can still get a shiny, nice-smelling car without breaking the bank by buying a car that's coming off a two- to three-year lease, or what is called an executive car (a fleet of cars that are used by car companies). That car is almost brand new, and we can buy it at a very good discount.

A car coming off a lease is typically in very good condition and doesn't have many miles on it. Because it's not pristine, though, you can buy it for a fraction of what it would cost to buy new.

I think about how much a new car will cost me in the long run. The car companies get us as they want us to focus on monthly payments. And they'll get those monthly payments down to us where we can afford it. We need to think instead about *annual* payments, and about the entire term of the loan.

If we're spending $500 a month for that car, that's $6,000 a year, not including the car insurance or the petrol. That could be two or three months of our income. Run the numbers, and then ask yourself, "Do I really need a car that nice, or could I buy a car that's less expensive—maybe a little older—but still looks good and still runs?"

Personal finance expert and star of *Shark Tank*, a popular TV show from ABC in the USA, Kevin O'Leary, also warns against buying a new car: "I use my phone to call Uber or Lyft, and they take me around the city. I save a fortune. I feel good about it," O'Leary says. "I hate cars."

And Suze Orman, who keeps her cars for 12 years or more, says to buy used and choose a model that you can afford over one that looks impressive. "One of the best ways to build financial security is to spend the least amount possible on a car that meets your needs," she wrote in a 2017 blog post. "Forget about the bells and whistles you want. Paying less helps you pay off the car faster."

Grow your income

After cutting many of my unnecessary expenses, I must grow my income to be unstoppable. Being "rich" means something different to everybody. For me, it means I'd never need to work again because I'd have enough income coming in off my investments. But after taking a break of two years, I've realised that I don't want to stop working. I just want to reinvent and reengineer myself. So what needs to change in my financial planning to accommodate those goals? It does not make sense to retire now, or even in my early 60s, if I am going to live to be 100. I need an active life.

A lesson from *Rich Dad, Poor Dad*: saving money is a horrible fallback plan, and certainly not a good one for retirement. There is nothing wrong with saving. It is better than blowing loads of money in gambling or on a new sports car. But it is not enough. In fact, anyone who plans to just work hard and save money is actually digging a financial grave. The truth is, savers are losers.

The fact that interest rates on savings today are so low only makes matters worse. Everything from high petrol cost and food prices to stock market booms and busts. Even the housing market can be traced back to this. Money just isn't worth what it used to be!

Savers are actually losing money through depreciation. So, what could I do instead? My answer: INVEST. And for my money, the absolute smartest and safest investment I know I can make today is in myself. Invest in my mind. The great thing is no one can take away what I have learned. They can take my business and take my stocks away, but I will just get them again because they can't take away my knowledge!

Unlike 20 to 30 years ago, anyone can become an investor today with a minimal investment fund. The invention of the internet has made it so that we can invest from home 24 hours a day. By becoming an investor, I become my own boss, or, better said, the boss of my money. My money is the thing working for me. It is my employee. I am able to gain more financial freedom, and my favourite part? I am able to get more TIME freedom.

As an investor, I get to create money—lots of it—instead of just saving it. Then, instead of the downward spiral of eroding my savings, invested money will be busy making more money.

In the past, I have learnt many investment methods, including FOREX, spread trading, stock and options trading, and real estate.

There are unlimited investment options for your portfolio. Personally, I am now focusing only on stocks. Historically, return rates are around 8-10% a year. Let's say I invest $500 per month at 8%, and I let that grow for 20 years. That is $296,000. I am inspired by the way Warren Buffett managed to turn $6,000 into $70billion using this long-term strategy of value investing!

After attending courses and doing my own research, I have three simple reasons for thinking highly of value investing. Anyone can do it. The philosophy behind value investing is incredibly simple:

- Research and buy undervalued stocks with a competitive and economic advantage

- Buy in with a margin of safety (stocks on sale)

- Hold stocks for long-term gains

I realised that as long as I am willing to learn, have patience, and get acquainted with my new best friend, a calculator, I can make it.

There is no emotion involved.

Emotions are poison to investing. It is normal to feel emotional pain when I lose money on stocks. Emotions also make me hate losing more than I like wining, which can lead to bad decisions.

An emotion-free approach to investing is really **helping** my portfolio.

Investment news travels around the world in seconds. I set my own personal rule in order not to fall into the trap of market watching. It is no coincidence that Warren Buffett, considered by many to be the greatest investor of all time, has no way to check stock quotes in his office. Buffett only does things that contribute to his long-term profitability, and reacting to every bit of news isn't one of them.

Compound interest

The plus of value investing is compound interest. Through the process of reinvesting my returns and dividends, my investments will keep growing exponentially. The power of compounding is one of Warren Buffett's success factors. He has been preaching this for six decades, it has made him a billionaire, and it is something that I must copy.

Before I buy anything, I have to answer the following questions: do I know this company's business model well enough to describe it to a ten year old? When I buy stock in a company, I am buying shares, or, literally, a portion of the company. I am a partner in a company. I would not become a partner in a business that I don't understand. I must have at least an idea of what the business is… and what success looks like. My rule is to keep it simple with the KISS test: *Keep it simple, stupid.*

Am I comfortable holding this stock for at least ten years? I am investing in stocks the same way as buying a private business. Owning requires more due diligence than renting. Renting makes me more likely to act on impulse and throw some money at something that catches my eye. After all, it is only for a short time. If I buy a house or car, though, I am likely to take a little more time to make sure it's something that I will be happy owning for a long time. This way, come bull or bear market, I will be just fine!

I aim to buy undervalued stocks that have strong financial conditions and are managed by people with skin in the game.

I don't look at my portfolio every day. This is simple, but plenty of research shows that the more people look at their portfolios, the worse their returns. This is probably because it makes them more likely to ditch something that has performed poorly or jump on something that looks like it is moving.

I don't own so much of any stock that it can kill me if it goes south.

Lots of older investors focus on stocks that pay generous dividends. That is a mistake. I focus on total return (capital gain plus dividends), not yield (dividend only).

In short, I believe if I am doing the right things, I have no reason to fear volatility or even a bear market. I need discipline to sit tight and stick to my plan.

But we all make mistakes, and you can learn from mine. You will hopefully make fewer mistakes. Here are the mistakes I made in the early days that I hope not to make again:

1. Thinking I knew more than the market. The market, like stocks, is an instant and ever-changing referendum on how millions of investors think about a particular asset. Even a single stock, an obscure market, or an edge at a certain time will not last.

2. Trusting stock insights from experts in the field or industry. I learnt this from listening to good friends who know the industry but not the stocks. I found the hard way that stock experts and industry experts are not the same.

3. Believing that my broker or relationship manager had my best financial interests in mind. I was stupid enough not

to know that the only person I should rely on to look after my money and my financial future is myself. Their "help" enriches them far more than it enriches me. Some or many of them made me poorer.

4. Believing that being rich is bad. This voice in my head stood in the way of my ever having much money. With money, I can help people in need where and how I can. I don't like to see inequality.

Before you jump into the investment world, you may want to watch a couple of movies like *The Big Short* or *Inside Job* for a lesson in the financial crises that affect us. *The Wolf of Wall Street* is the best portrait of greed of the late 2000s, and the glorification of it that led to ruin. This will be a good reminder for you when you invest.

Let me share with you a success story of Kelly or Takorn Waraprissopon of fintelligence.co.th, who I met two years ago when we both attended a seminar in Bangkok.

I grew up in a middle-class family. I had a dream of being financially free. I worked two jobs simultaneously for 15 years, as I believed that hard work would make me reach my financial goal faster.

I climbed high up the corporate ladder. I earned a high pay, but worked like two dogs. It drove me to lose my life balance, my health, and time with family. I almost had an accident on the way home one day due to extreme exhaustion. I needed to replace my source of income, and that's why I reopened my mind to the investment world again.

When I was younger, I lost all my five years of savings in just six days. I was looking for quick returns, and every investment I made was speculation. I kept praying for stock prices to go up. It sounds silly, but the truth is that I didn't even know what kind of businesses I was investing in.

I believe that one must have the right investing knowledge to succeed. By reading and attending lots of investment seminars, I learnt from many value investors and some famous investors such as Dr. Niwes Hemvachiravarakorn—the Warren Buffett of Thailand—and Mary Buffett—Warren Buffett's former daughter-in-law. I also learned from Sean Seah, a self-made millionaire who learned from Mary Buffett. He is my mentor, business partner, and best friend.

Then I turned my knowledge into action. I read company profiles and financial statements. I'm happy when I see customers queueing to pay or buy things from the companies I've invested in, as it means more revenue and more chance for net profit growth. I don't have to worry about stock prices going up ever again. Sometimes, stock prices go down, but as long as revenue and profit grow and business fundamentals are strong, the price will match its intrinsic value.

After spending years investing, my portfolio is growing consistently. Now, my investment results allow me to spend time with my family, do what I love, and enjoy good health.

The concept of value investing is very simple, but it's a big challenge to apply. You need to fight with a lot of noise and greed when you see others making quick money and you haven't seen any return; however, value investing helps you last in the market. So be patient: investing is about lifetime security, not quick money.

I started with a huge failure, so I want to help prevent people from falling into the same trap I did. I want to spread the right knowledge so no one else has to waste their time. Now I spread out my knowledge and experience to thousands of people. I believe that this will help them succeed faster and make more profit than I ever did.

Value investing can be applied to any purchase

When deciding whether to invest in a company, billionaire Warren Buffett looks for businesses that will continue to have a competitive advantage decades down the line. Simply put, Buffett decides a business is worth investing in because it will last, not because it's doing well right now. He purchased See's Candies with longtime business partner Charlie Munger in 1972, and spent more than $1billion on Coca-Cola stock in 1988—both of which turned out to be good bets, and both of which he still owns today.

"Put together a portfolio of companies whose aggregate earnings march upward over the years, and so also will the portfolio's market value," Buffett wrote in his 1996 letter to shareholders. "If you aren't willing to own a stock for ten years, don't even think about owning it for ten minutes."

While not everyone will garner the same results as Buffett on the stock market, his core principle can be applied to almost every purchase we make: invest for the long-term.

When deciding whether or not to buy a home, one of the first questions to ask yourself is, "How long do I plan on staying here?" The longer you live there, usually the more valuable your purchase will become. The same goes for clothing, appliances, furniture, and anything else that I use on a daily basis. While it's tempting to skimp and get the cheapest option, especially if I am on a tight budget, over time nicer items may hold up better, making the initial outlay worth it.

Now, I kind of do this method: I hold it in my hands. Or, if I'm shopping online, I don't typically buy something when I first see it. I will just look at it. If I still want it in two weeks, then I'll get it. There are a few exceptions, but for a bigger purchase, I'll sit on it for a while and mull it over. A lot of times, the feeling of, "Oh I just have to have this" passes.

Plenty of companies will game us to buy something right away, but that doesn't mean it's going to bring you any peace, satisfaction, or happiness. Instead, just sit on it. If it's not sticking with you *before* you get it, it's not actually going to add to your life *when* you get it.

Think of it in terms of cost per use. For example, say I invest in a $200 blazer from a high-end store. If it's a wardrobe staple and I wear it twice a week for the whole year, that's 104 days of wear. Divide the cost, $200, by the number of days, and I end up under $2 per wear. Not a bad deal, especially if I feel great in it.

When I'm shopping for a new pair of jeans or am in the market for a new car, I apply the Buffett rule: is this something worth holding onto?

If the master of value investing serves as any example, the discipline to buy things only when I really, really like them pays off.

Real estate

Many of my friends and family prefer real estate investments. They all started small and grew with time. To me, real estate must produce cash flow, like single-family houses, an apartment, condo, retail stores, etc. Their reason to enter into real estate is to create an ongoing stream of income, and, if the value of the property goes up, to catch the profit, or appreciation, by selling.

Cash flow and appreciation are two forms of revenue from rental properties. This is good for anyone with patience, as it is typical for long-term play. A cash flow property is not subject to the daily ups and downs of the market.

However, for me, I am not keen as it is not liquid. I simply can't jump in and out of real estate very quickly, making it difficult to convert the asset into cash in a hurry. One particular reason for me is that real estate is the second most difficult endeavour (after business). Properties must be managed on a daily basis, including vacancies and bad tenants.

Own a business

I love the *Rich Dad* teaching on the cash flow quadrant. The cash flow quadrant says there are four types of people in the world of business, money, and stocks: employees, self-employed, business owners, and investors.

The *Rich Dad* messages and philosophies are designed to help anyone leave the employee and self-employed quadrants and enter the big business and investor quadrants.

The big business owner quadrant is where systems are king. They are big because they make a lot of money through systems, not because they have a lot of employees. Today, most businesses have software and processes that do almost all the work, relying on automation and technology.

Business owners pay some of the lowest percentages in taxes, and most importantly, have the freest time and money. They control their own lives. This is success.

People in the investor quadrant make money with money. They don't have to work because their money is working for them. The investor quadrant is the playground of the rich.

That was a good lesson for me, and I got inspired by the story of Vishen Lakhiani, the founder of Mindvalley University. He has called himself a mediocre entrepreneur who previously got shot down when he tried to get funding, yet he used $700 to build a company that is now, after 15 years, home to more than three million students and numerous accolades.

The effort to start each of my businesses was Herculean, to say the least. Every new business meant I would spend years building, marketing, and monetising from the ground up. But I thrive on a challenge, and the chance to help people in the growing world of online community is irresistible.

My key is to get out of the old rules of business and build a sustainable and lasting business from the foundation of my experience, interest, and personality. A business that is focused on service to others is a sure way to success as an entrepreneur in the long run.

Gold

One particular investment will do better than most should another crisis hit: gold (physical gold, not paper gold). I include gold as portfolio insurance. Its correlation with all of the world's major stock markets is very low. In 2008, when the S&P 500 dropped 38%, and the global financial system teetered on the brink of collapse, gold prices climbed 6%. In other words, a well diversified portfolio should include gold, kept in a safe place (not at home or in a bank safe deposit box).

Passive income

Making money while you sleep has a nice ring to it, doesn't it? After reading books like *Rich Dad, Poor Dad* and *The 4-Hour Work Week*, I became obsessed with making passive income.

Whenever someone needs additional income, the stereotypical solution is to get a part-time job. But what if you don't have the time or energy to put in all those extra hours? I know I didn't. Plus, that wasn't as appealing as making money while I was trading time for money.

Passive income is the Holy Grail for online marketers. It's automatic. Effortless. But not at first. In the beginning, it's gruelling. I liken this to doing the most amount of work for the least initial return. However, over time, as your passive income begins to increase, your reliance on an active income plummets. That's when the real magic starts to happen.

For most people, that means an exit from the proverbial rat race. It means freedom. True financial independence. An extrication from the shackles that bind us to the 9-to-5 life-sucking job. It means being unleashed. Living a fulfilled life. And having total freedom to live, work, and roam free at your leisure. That's by design. But, if you're sitting there thinking that passive income is impossible because you're too busy working a day job, think again. Not only is it possible—not only *should* you do it—but you'd be silly not to put as much of your effort into generating a passive income immediately.

However, this comes back to the old discussion of pain versus pleasure. We will always do more to avoid pain than we will to gain pleasure. When our backs are against the wall, we act. When they're not, we relax. The truth is that the pain-versus-pleasure paradigm operates only in the short term. We'll only avoid pain in the here and now. Often not in the long term.

But passive income isn't that hard to generate. When you know what avenue to take, and you follow a few simple steps, you can do it. It just takes time. Don't expect this to materialise overnight. Unless, of course, you have money to invest in something like real estate or high-yield dividend stocks.

There are dozens of ways to generate passive income. The option you select has to do with two metrics: time and money. Either you have a lot of time or a lot of money. Most people usually don't have both. If you have a lot of money, generating passive income almost instantly is easy. You can buy up some real estate and begin enjoying rental income. Or, you can invest in a dividend or index fund or some other investment vehicle that will begin generating a steady income for you.

However, when you lack the money, you need time. You'll need to invest the time now in order to reap the benefits of automatic income later. It doesn't happen overnight, so don't expect it to. However, you can do this without quitting your day job. All it takes is some sincere effort over a consistent period.

There is that popular business concept, the Pareto principle, that says 80% of your results come from 20% of your time and effort. 20% of your time and effort produces 80% of your results, which is one fifth of your time. You may want to consider that if you spend five times as much time and effort on your most valuable activities, you will increase your results by 400% or four times (5x80% = 400%). To sum up, when you are able to live and work according to your purpose and passion with 100% of the time or 80% of your time rather than 5-20% of your time like when you started, it will bring you to new life fulfilment, and your business and revenue will soar. There is always something you could do, but if it is taking you away from your purpose and passion, it is not worth it.

For that, create space for it and stick with the difficulty at the beginning until it becomes comfortable. You may need some passive income ideas—ways to make money with a little investment of time and effort on your part. You might make YouTube videos, put your photography to work on the web, write a book/e-book or blog, sell products on the internet, build an app, create an online course, or build an online guide.

Create your own economy

I like what Tony Robbins says: "To really get yourself on the road to financial freedom, the first step is deciding you are no longer just going to be a consumer. You are going to be an owner.

You have got to decide, *Instead of being the chess piece, I am going to become the chess player.*"

I notice that a lot of people, especially those in the younger generations, are taking the future of work into their own hands. They are sharing resources and technology, taking gigs through job sites, creating freelance businesses, and innovating methods of generating income. They are applying their experiences in new ways, learning new skills, and tapping into endless resources for training and support. They are designing their lives, carving out time for family, and building professions based on their passions. They are living the way they want, doing the things they want, and making as much money as they want.

Entrepreneurship has existed for thousands of years, and the idea of part-time work to supplement a primary income is not new. But these ingredients alone were not enough to spur the new revolution. It is a specific mix of technology, timing, and economic evolution. We are all responding to the rise of the peer-to-peer business model. For example, I get supermarket and meal deliveries through an app on my phone. It seems more and more people get into this service for both sides. Thanks to online purchasing power and the technology of GPS, people with visions of an innovative marketplace can make those visions come to life. As an individual, I am now able to do what only large corporations could do 20 years ago.

The key is attitude. When someone believes they can do it, it becomes a self-fulfilling prophecy. From side hustle opportunities, freelance gigs, and shared ways of earning money, the options for increasing income are endless.

Once you have the right attitude, know your purpose, consider your passion, and evaluate your skill sets. Living with purpose means doing what we love, what we are most gifted at, what we are passionate about, and what feeds our energy. It is the thing we may do if we are not paid. However, you may need to bolster this with additional training. The good news is that there are opportunities available, and a lot of the risk that used to be associated with taking control of your career has been removed. By offering side gigs that create a steady build-up of income, you could gradually make the leap into a full-time independent life. Direct selling and franchise operations offer support through companies proven in their industries. Freelancers and entrepreneurs alike find educational and personal development through a number of resources. To discover your purpose, you can start by asking yourself some questions: where am I happiest? What does an ideal life look like? What are the things I am most passionate about in life? What activities did I excel in during my younger days?

Answering these questions will bring you closer to discovering your purpose. But, even after serious thought, the answer may not be there. I took the Myers-Briggs personality test to identify my talents, my instincts, and the ways that I couldn't see myself. It was an incredible exercise to learn how to work with my strengths instead of against them. Alternatively, you can ask a few people who know you best about the one thing they think you do really well. You may be surprised by the answers.

Financial planning

I update my net worth twice yearly. The formula is simple: assets (all I own) minus liabilities (all I owe). It is not the most exciting activity of my day, but it is worth the effort. The net worth statement is like my progress report. It is a snapshot of what I have done so far, identifying where I am earning an A-plus and where I need to turn in missed assignments and do some extra credit. Creating and maintaining my net worth statement will:

- Give me a list of all my assets and investments

- Provide crucial information when using a retirement calculator

- Determine whether my emergency fund is sufficient

I include only assets that could be sold or converted into cash relatively easily such as homes, investment properties, cars, art, jewellery and other valuable possessions, investments, businesses that I own or have an ownership interest in, and cash (saving accounts, checking accounts, etc.).

Liabilities are pretty straightforward. Unlike assets, most liabilities are set in stone. Debts take many forms, but some common liabilities I include in my net worth calculation are mortgages, car loans, bank and personal loans (if any), and credit card debt (no more).

As the value of my assets (especially my home and investments) increases and I pay off my debts, my future net worth is increased fairly consistently; therefore, it is a good habit to calculate a personal balance sheet every so often. If twice a year is difficult, aim for once a year to track overall financial progress and take action.

The value in measuring financial health

Most people are struggling financially because most people lack financial health! This has a real impact on our lives and our ability to weather life's inevitable ups and downs.

For financial health, I can put the story into four components: spend, save, borrow, and plan. These components mirror our daily financial activities. What we do today in terms of spending, saving, borrowing, and planning either builds toward or detracts from our resilience and ability to pursue opportunities. For example, will we be able to handle a car breakdown or an extra medical bill? Will we be able to save for any of our dreams?

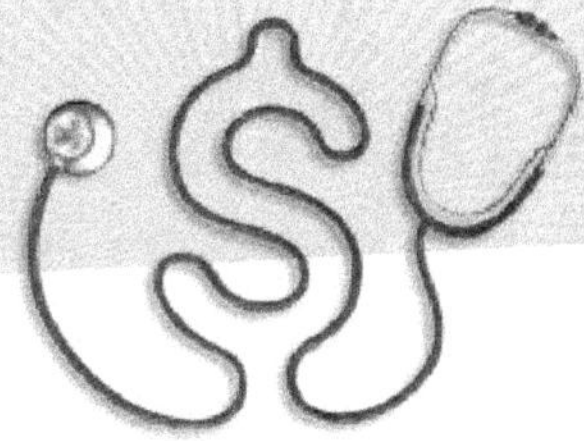

Components of financial health

- have sufficient living expenses in liquid savings for many months
- have sufficient long-term savings or assets

- have a sustainable debt-to-income ratio
- have a good credit score or credit tier

FINANCIAL HEALTH

- spend less than income
- pay bills on time and in full

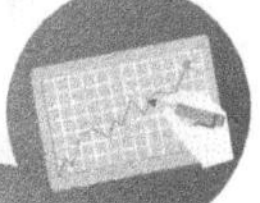

- have appropriate insurance
- plan ahead for expenses

Finance habits

Now you know a few principles for you to follow so you can create wealth and reach high levels of financial success. It will not be easy and some keys to create new habits—that I learnt the hard way—are below:

Step out of your comfort zone - success is not a straight line, the road to success is filled with many twists and turns. Adapting to unexpected events is one key factor to achieve any big goal in life. When you feel lost, confused or frustrated, the steps to take are to move outside your comfort zone which will move you ahead by doing things differently.

Come out with specific money goals - write down goals for your annual income and net worth. Like all goal setting, be realistic but don't be afraid to challenge yourself. After all, the wealthiest people are not afraid to think big.

Focus on expanding - instead of looking for reasons why everything is wrong, pay attention to what's right. When you focus on your goals in a different way, you will find new roads opening up that you did not notice before.

Automate your finances - send money automatically to investment accounts, savings accounts, and others. This will allow you to build wealth effortlessly. Start investing sooner rather than later rather to take full advantage of compound interest. The miracle of compounding can transform a relatively small but consistent amount of saving into major wealth. Get into the habit of putting any surprise cash such as a bonus, birthday money or even just a $20 bill you found to work. This habit will help you avoid lifestyle inflation.

> *"Compound interest is the eighth wonder of the world. He who understands it, earns it. He who doesn't, pays it."*
> *— Albert Einstein*

Model rich and successful people - I studied the people who are rich and successful. I learnt what it takes and how they got there. I read their books, biographies, etc. I found out how they progressed from where they were to where they are today. Then, I modelled my approach after theirs.

For value investing, I really like to follow InvestED Podcast by Phil Town, ruleoneinvesting.com who teams up with his daughter, Danielle Town. Their book *Invested : How Warren Buffett and Charlie Munger Taught Me to Master My Mind, My Emotions, and My Money (with a Little Help from My Dad)* is what I really recommend anyone who wants to enter into value investing to read.

For investment, I love this book, *The Dhandho Investor: The Low-risk Value Method to High Returns* by Mohnish Pabrai.

There are many more books and podcasts that are really good and can inspire us to make progress. These are ones that really helped me to reduce any wrong steps by learning from someone who has done it before.

Focus on solving problems instead of focusing on money – the rich get wealthy by building businesses that solve problems for others. We need to shift our focus to being a problem solver. Money is a result of helping others and providing value to their lives.

Never stop learning.

> *"Life is like riding a bicycle. To keep your balance you must keep moving."*
> *– Albert Einstein*

Stay humble and keep on learning to get better every day. Those who fall into the trap of being a know-it-all will not be successful. For investment, I keep on learning from books and podcasts.

Apart from InvestED, I also listen to The Rich Dad Radio Show with Robert Kiyosaki, The Science of Economic Freedom by Doug Fabian, Master of Scale with Reid Hoffman and Motley Fool Money.

Surround yourself with successful and high-earning people—successful people generally agree that consciousness is contagious, and that exposure to people who are more successful has the potential to expand your thinking and catapult your income. We become like the people we associate with, and that's why winners are attracted to winners.

> **"You're The Average Of The Five People You Spend The Most Time With."**
> **– Jim Rohn**

FeelGoodX - Finances Manifesto

I always pay myself first no matter what.

I put money into my accounts automatically.

I create my life and excell in managing my wealth towards my values and goals.

I believe money is important to have freedom and make life more enjoyable.

I make my money work hard for me to make me more and more money.

My wealth comes from doing what I love. I create part-time businesses to create passive income streams. I am an excellent receiver with gratitude.

I am a generous giver and add value to other people's lives.

I am grateful for all the money I have now. But I expand my capacity to earn, hold, and grow money daily.

FEELGOODX

LIVE YOUR LIFE, LOVE YOUR LIFE

Home and environment

A house is built of wall and beams, a home is built of love and dreams.

Right now, in our home, there are things that signal another to-do item on our list. But lately, rather than sigh over the decay of our pristine home, we have been learning to embrace *wabi-sabi*, the Japanese art of appreciating the beauty in the naturally imperfect world.

Wabi-sabi is an ancient aesthetic philosophy rooted in Zen Buddhism, particularly the tea ceremony. This is a ritual of purity and simplicity, in which masters prized bowls that were handmade and irregularly shaped with uneven glaze, cracks, and a perverse beauty in their deliberate imperfection. There is no direct western translation for *wabi-sabi*, but essentially it is the art of finding beauty in the imperfect, impermanent, and incomplete.

It is fair to say that, in the past, my wife and I were obsessed with perfection, as we always wanted to have perfectly matching everything in our home. Authenticity is a big part of *wabi-sabi*, so imperfections are cherished for symbolising the passage of time and loving use. Embracing *wabi-sabi* in our home teaches us to be content with our current lot without constantly yearning for more. It is the perfect antidote to a throwaway society built on disposable goods and mass-produced homogeneous items.

A *wabi-sabi* approach to life is not about giving way to carelessness or seeing a junk pile through rose-coloured glasses. It is about appreciating, showcasing, and sustaining the beauty of what's natural. Like wine: a perfect wine is too obvious. I am far less drawn to genetic, technically correct wines than to wines with complexity, even if that complexity comes with a whiff of fault.

Design trends can come from just about anywhere. In our case, we have a 15th-century Japanese philosophy to thank for bringing us *wabi-sabi*. In our minds, it is all about embracing imperfection and personal authenticity, and then going deeper and celebrating that reality. We used to be tempted to constantly add new things to our home, but *wabi-sabi* is all about stripping back the unnecessary to allow ourselves to live well. We consider getting rid of superfluous clutter by ridding ourselves of pointless items. By doing this, we allow the things that really matter to stand out and shine. Every object in our home must be beautiful, useful, or both.

We have shifted our perspective from one of perfecting to one of appreciating. Embracing *wabi-sabi* helps create a pleasant environment at home. By falling in love with our imperfect home and possessions, we reduce the need to buy many new things. This reduces consumption, which saves money and puts less strain on our planet.

Our mindset has changed, too. *Wabi-sabi* puts the focus on gratitude for what we already have rather than on always yearning for something new and shiny. This powerful shift in perspective helps us to feel more peaceful and content in the current moment, and by doing so, allows us to embrace serenity and tranquility in our day-to-day lives.

Beyond our home, *wabi-sabi* offers a useful framework for modern life in general, finding beauty in the imperfect, appreciating nature, and striving for contentment.

Clutter

One of the main activities after adopting *wabi-sabi* is to clear the clutter. Just like we get caught up in the expectations of others, we can get caught up in material possessions that distract us from our internal needs. We started getting rid of items, gifts, or even big pieces of furniture that we were holding onto, and instead donated them to someone in need. We cleaned away things in the home that caused anxiety and got rid of clothes we had not touched for a long time. A more organised and simplified space helped us focus on more meaningful and non-material aspects of life, helping our spirits shine brighter.

We followed declutter guru Marie Kondo's KonMari method, in which tidying is not just cleaning our home, but also a way to become better decision-makers, live healthier, and reach our dreams. The purpose of tidying isn't just to keep things clean and organised. Rather, our goal is to create a space that improves our bodies and minds. The six basic rules of tidying, according to her method are: 1) commit yourself to tidying up, 2) imagine your ideal lifestyle, 3) finish discarding first, 4) tidy by category, not by location, 5) follow the right order, 6) ask yourself if it sparks joy.

This is where the power of tidying lies, much like meditation. Its lasting effects come from doing what feels right for our environment, our belongings, and, ultimately, our wellbeing. In fact, we see tidying our living space as a way of detoxing our body and mind.

We began the process of tidying, starting with the easiest categories like clothes, books, documents, and miscellaneous items, and ended with our sentimental items. We aimed for simplicity and visual order when organising what we kept. We took time to consider carefully how we felt whenever we used or looked at our belongings in the spaces we had designated for them. Efficient and intuitive storage eliminates the stress of having to search through clutter for the thing we need. It allows us to make decisions instead of being stuck searching helplessly for hours.

The process of tidying was exhausting, and we spent a lot of time on this journey. Our key vision was to declutter our lives, which should have been extremely simple. All we had to do was decide what we wanted to keep and discard what we didn't. To accomplish this, we had to dig deep to figure out what kind of life we wanted to live. It is always up to us to develop the kind of space that reflects our ideal future.

We made tidying a more enjoyable experience by putting on our favourite playlist and visualising how much better we would feel in our new space. We learnt to express gratitude for items that we were getting rid of. This helps us to acknowledge the purpose and utility of everything, treat our belongings with respect, and be more critical of the new stuff we allow into our home. Lastly, my wife would keep saying that it should be everyone's responsibility to keep it clean. She would say things like, "We are living together, so it is important to maintain our space."

Cleaning and tidying are daily tasks, and what matters most is consistency. Even a short amount of time will do, so get into the habit of making a reasonable effort to clean and tidy up every day. As soon as we finish using something, we put it away. If we are meticulous about tidiness, there will never be anything just scattered around. This may not be easily accomplished, but at least we try to return things we have used or made a mess of to their rightful places before the day is over. It is important that our home is tidy so we can kick off the next morning feeling refreshed. At first, it was hard to develop the habit, but once we got into it, we felt our bodies and minds being refreshed each day. As Kondo said, this is the first step in getting the rest of our life in order too.

Feng shui

Feng shui, literally translated as "wind and water," is an ancient Chinese art from over 4,000 years ago. It has been used to create greater health, wealth, and happiness, and is the practice of arranging the environment so that energy, or chi, flows gently and smoothly through our home or business.

In this way, our space just feels good and supports what we want out of life, whether that's a better career, romance, health, or income.

Feng shui is created by organising an environment in a way that enhances the flow of chi. Chi is life-giving energy that unites our body, mind, and spirit.

Just as chi flows through our body, chi also flows through the living environment. When the energy flow is stagnant, the unbalanced chi may lead to ill health, domestic strife, or financial concerns.

Feng shui adjustments help make sure that the chi energy flow is just right so that everything in our environment supports our wish for good luck, good health, harmonious relationships, and prosperity.

Together with my wife, we have discussed with many Feng shui consultants from different countries. Recently, my wife decided to learn the practice for herself. I followed her to live classes of Dato' Joey Yap which always had a few thousand attendees eager to learn more. Here is my summary:

First of all, Feng shui is not about the art of placement, nor is it about interior design. Man-made objects do not generate chi or cosmic energy on their own. Classical Feng shui is about focusing on the alignment of chi from the natural environment based on direction, location, time, land formation, and water formation.

Feng shui is an art of assessing quality of life through observing and analysing an individual's living environment. It is the serious study of how the unseen energies in our living environment affect the people living or working there.

Feng shui is practical. Its aim is to improve quality of life, not dictate taste in décor or artwork. Things should be kept as natural as possible. After all, if the chi is good, no further cure or embellishments are needed. Practise common sense when it comes to interior decorating and design, and learn to tell the difference between a psychological effect and a Feng shui one.

Let's go through what we learnt with a few key points for building a home with good Feng shui:

In Feng shui, there is no such thing as a house that is unworkable. Every home can implement Feng shui, and some better than others, but don't let what you can't do stop you from doing what you can.

Pay attention to the surroundings. If the chi entering a property from the environment is negative, we can't cure it. All we can do is prevent the chi from entering the house, leaving us in a neutral situation.

Having a home next to any of these is a major bonus:

Mountains or hills, even small ones. Having a house with its back toward the mountains would be best, but even mountains at the side of the house is fine.

Having a natural, smooth-flowing water source nearby is always good. However, don't confuse this with man-made water sources like swimming pools or artificial lakes.

An open space like a park or a field in front, which collects chi.

Location in a quiet and peaceful neighbourhood.

Avoid buying homes located near any of these:

- A highway or a road that has constant traffic.

- A train or monorail line. If the unit is above the track or highway, the negative impact of these features is lessened.

- A drain cut right in front of the house, as this completely blocks the chi flow into the house.

- A garbage dump or a construction site. It could be temporary, but while it is present, the negative features are quite harsh.

- A tall sharp object, such as a pylon or water tower

- A sharp edge pointing toward the house, such as the corner of a roof

- An alleyway, T-junction, or other roads

Here are a few simple tips for inside the house:

The main door is one of the major features of a home that must be evaluated. If there is a tall structure like a lamppost near the main door, it can affect health and career. Avoid houses with narrow gaps between other houses visible from the main door, and also avoid thick foliage over the main door or shadows cast over the property in general. This can cause mental health problems.

The kitchen represents life and health. A badly located kitchen usually indicates poor health for the residents. The kitchen should always be toward the side of the house, as locating a kitchen in the centre creates instability and long-term health problems.

The bedrooms should be located in suitable sectors, and the rooms should be in the shape of a square, as this can help cut off negative chi that impacts the room.

Feng shui is a vast subject that requires years to fully understand. The information here is just the tip of the iceberg, but it shows that Feng shui can be easily implemented.

Pollution inside the home

Outside air is probably safer than the air in our home, even if you live in a highly polluted city like Bangkok! Why? Because chemicals from things like kitchen cleaner, air freshener, pesticides, printer ink, paint, and even dish soap make up about half of what is polluting our air. And every time we clean the counters, spritz perfumes, or paint our living room walls, the fumes are getting trapped in our home, thanks to insulated walls and the roof over our head.

I have researched a few things we can do to protect ourselves from pollutants that are lurking around our homes:

1. Check the "fine print" first. Now, there are a lot of options for products on the market. Some are "greener" than others. But many common stain removers, dish soaps, and laundry detergents are loaded with scary chemicals that we don't suspect. Things

like formaldehyde and methanol—the same substances that are used in embalming fluids! Not only that, but these chemicals are known to cause all sorts of health problems, like asthma, burning eyes and airways, nausea, skin irritation, and serious illness. Plus, these chemicals go by many names, so if we don't see it in the ingredient list, it does not mean we are in the clear.

I look at the small print to be sure that I am getting a safer option. If a household item has any warning on it, that can be a sure-fire way to figure out if it is good or bad. According to the US National Safety Council, here is what to keep an eye out for:

- Caution: these products have the lowest level of potential harm. They're not great, but they're not the most dangerous stuff out there. These are the best commercial options.

- Warning: anything with a warning label carries more risk. We could become seriously ill or injured by this product. Avoid these ones, if possible, but they are still better options than anything below.

- Danger: red alert! "Danger" has the highest risk. It can cause skin damage or worse.

Overall, I think it is best to avoid any product that says, "Harmful if swallowed."

2. Kitchen and bathroom cleaners can be a huge health hazard. Researchers have found all sorts of side effects—everything from increased breathing problems to allergies to being poisoned from mixing cleaners!

Actually, we can make our own cleaners. A mild solution of vinegar and water will work just fine. Researchers have known for years about the cleaning power of vinegar. Simply mix equal parts vinegar with tap water, spray it directly on any hard surface, and wipe clean with a rag. Sometimes, I even use straight vinegar to do spot cleaning. It is stronger, so the scent is powerful, but that will go away as it dries. It is definitely better than the chemicals in most cleaners.

3. It is not realistic to get rid of all our household products. After all, they are a part of modern life. So until they are made in a safer way, we take precautions to protect ourselves by getting some indoor plants. Plants filter the air and get rid of some of these nasty chemicals. It is worth keeping some low-maintenance plants around the home. Plants absorb not only carbon dioxide but also gases and chemicals in the air. In exchange, they add oxygen and even healthy moisture levels to the environment. On top of that, they are beautiful and bring a little of the outdoors in. Just a caution: some indoor houseplants have toxic properties and are not ideal to have around small children and pets. Some plants that can purify the air and are relatively easy to find are ferns, aloe vera, snake plants, and mother-in-law's tongue.

Apart from these, we practise a few habits for a greener home:

- Conserve water. Water is a precious, natural, valuable resource, and we can help by conserving it.

- Unplug electronics when they are not in use. 23% of all the energy that comes into our homes goes into devices that are not turned off. By unplugging those devices, we are going to save a lot of energy and money.

- Cut back on TV time. Not too many people will tell us that watching TV is healthy, and more and more research has begun validating what we already know.

- Change light bulbs to LED lighting, which is 75% more efficient and the bulbs last much longer.

Home humidity

As I live in a tropical country, I live in a high-humidity environment, especially during the rainy season. I spoke to my former colleague who is an expert in engineering, and he told me that humidity is actually a huge indicator of the health of our home. If it does not run below the 60% range, we run the risk of breathing air that is either too dry, which could cause respiratory irritation, or too damp, which means hello mould! Just because we don't see it does not mean it is not there.

With that, my wife went on to search for more information and found that black mould is not the only one we should worry about. It turns out there are a lot of different species of mould that could grow at home. White mould can survive at between 60-70% humidity, and black mould requires about 90% humidity to grow.

That means it is a good idea to invest in a portable humidity metre that you can carry around your whole home. It will only set you back around $10 to $20. When a room's humidity is approaching the danger zone, we use a small dehumidifier to bring it back down to normal levels. There are many options on the market these days; just keep in mind that some are noisier than others if you are placing it in a bedroom.

Living in Bangkok, we never experience the feeling of "not humid enough," but we had that experience when we lived in Dalian. It was not dangerous, but it was just plain uncomfortable and could lead to respiratory irritation, dehydration, and the like.

Environment

> *"It is our collective and individual responsibility to preserve and tend to the world in which we all live."*
> *—Dalai Lama*

Global warming is already presenting us with a fair share of health problems. For instance, as climate change worsens, air quality is decreasing, leading to a rise in respiratory disease and spurring an increase in vector-related illnesses such as mosquito-borne diseases transmitted through food and water. Rising sea levels are forcing the first wave of climate refugees to flee their flooded homes. Climate change is spurring extreme weather events that are destroying our food, water, and shelter. These are just the health challenges we are already experiencing, and more are likely coming.

Climate change will affect the way we continue to thrive on this planet. We want life for us and future generations to be more about success than survival. It is time to fight for our Mother Earth because there is no Planet B.

Improving health and our earth via green habits

While it is true that practices such as not buying products in plastic packaging, recycling, and taking shorter showers are part of a sustainable lifestyle, there are other ways to live a green life. It is important to understand that sustainability has other aspects, and the tips below can help habits in order to help the planet and you.

We avoid single-use items. One great way to eliminate waste is by boycotting various disposable items. If you need to use a straw, buy reusable straws, and bring your own tumbler for coffee.

Buy foods that use little to no packaging whenever possible, and use reusable lunch boxes instead of single-use plastic wrap and bags. If more people stopped patronising single-use convenience items, we could help reduce plastic waste around the globe.

Going paperless is another effective way of eliminating waste. About seven years ago, I made my bank statements and household bills electronic. Instead of buying papers or magazines, I read them in electronic form or PDF. If I do end up with newspapers in my home, I recycle them to clean windows. We have been actively taking out items that we have not been using and donating them. By giving new life to old things, we can help halt the production of disposable and single-use products.

> *"What we are doing to the forests of the world is but a mirror reflection of what we are doing to ourselves and to one another."*
> *—Mahatma Gandhi*

PART C: Soul
LIVE YOUR LIFE,
LOVE YOUR LIFE

FEELGOODX
LIVE YOUR LIFE, LOVE YOUR LIFE

Mindset and practices

It is admirable to be in control of myself in tense situations. Such measured behaviour is not my natural temperament. When I was younger, and even just a few years ago, I was hot-headed and volatile; my reactions to situations were not always calm. But my wife has helped me to become a master of measured responses in tricky situations. Being sometimes dull with self-control is better than passionate flare-ups.

I was an impatient person, and I wanted things to be done immediately. I have mistaken impulsive behaviour for "quick thinking" and being proactive. But good decisions are not based on speed—they are based on direction. Accurately calculating the direction my decision will take further down the line requires a long-sighted perspective, not impatience and impulsiveness.

> *"I have just three things to teach: simplicity, patience, compassion. These three are your greatest treasures."*
> *—Lao Tzu*

I used to have a rigid black-and-white ideology. But now, I always carefully consider not only both sides of the coin, but also the option in between. For most issues, this helps me to see many shades of grey in between black and white extremes. This encourages sympathy with many perspectives, an ability to compromise, and a sensitivity that brings me close to what is usually called wisdom.

I was not born naturally courageous. From an early age, I knew that I was not fearless. Fear was something I had to learn to deal with.

Being courageous is a choice, and it was during my time in military service camp that I first made this choice. There was one exercise that I could not do due to fear. This humiliating experience convinced me that I was not born courageous, but I promised myself that I would never again falter; I would learn to conquer my fears.

Conquering fears means looking strong even when I am afraid. Pretending to be brave. I became successful in my career simply by always appearing courageous.

Courage is a choice, and everyone can be courageous. It doesn't mean risking my life. It means learning to cope with my anxieties and fears every day. My ability to hide my fear was calming and comforting to many of my team members; it is my way of developing good leadership habits.

> **"Wisdom, compassion, and courage are the three universally recognised mortal qualities of men."**
> **—Confucius**

A book that changed my attitude is *Mindset* by Carol Dweck. This book discusses the difference between people with a fixed mindset versus those with a growth mindset. Our mindset determines the way we deal with tough situations and setbacks, as well as our willingness to deal with and improve ourselves.

The key message I learnt from this book is that people with a fixed mindset obstruct their own development through their belief in innate talent and their fear of failure. On the contrary, people with a growth mindset work hard and train hard to ultimately realise their potential to the fullest. By confronting our attitudes and ideas, we can develop a growth mindset.

Our mindset has an effect on our behaviour. People with a fixed mindset seek approval. Those with a growth mindset seek development. The fixed mindset sees failures as disasters; the growth mindset sees them as opportunities. People with a fixed mindset avoid difficulties, while those with a growth mindset relish them.

Our mindset is often strongly influenced by the role models we had as children, but anyone can adopt a growth mindset and make the impossible possible.

After reading *Mindset*, I embarked on a journey. It started by accepting that I have both mindsets. Then I learnt to recognise what triggers my fixed mindset. Failure? Criticism? Deadlines? Disagreements?

From there, I came to understand what happens to me when my fixed mindset "persona" is triggered. What is this persona? What is its name? What does it make me think, feel, and do? How does it affect those around me? Importantly, I gradually learned to remain in a growth mindset place despite the triggers, as I educated my persona and invited it to join me on my growth-mindset journey.

Here is a story about triggering my fixed mindset and its impact:

Meet Humin, my histrionic fixed mindset persona. He sneaks into my subconscious and undermines me. The name Humin(s) is a class of insoluble organic compounds. They are generally undesirable! They reflect his insistence on unwavering, natural strength. He detests delay, second place, and imperfections. Any whiff of delay, failure, or imperfection can trigger Humin's entrance. He comes forth when I get criticised or experience failure, causing me to become defensive and he is quick to blame others to preserve his ego. He rejects failure instead of embracing it. Humin convinces me that failure is definitive. Mistakes can take away my future success.

It was tough to change, but it was worth it. My life has been enhanced, and how I feel now is different than before. I have a richer life, and I am a more alive, courageous, and open person because of it. A change to a growth mindset did not solve all my problems, and I continue to embark on fixing more areas, thanks to my growth mindset.

Our mindset also determines our health. Stress levels in our culture have hit epidemic proportions, and we need to learn how to deal with stress in order to break free from its negative effects. Meditation, prayer, yoga, Tai Chi, and art can be very helpful, as long as we develop the right perspective and use it to help clear our minds better. We all dream of being whisked to some tropical island where all our stress can go away, but the truth is most of life's problems are awaiting us upon our return. So what happened on holiday that helps so much? Well, we separate from our normal routine and allow the mind to refresh and rejuvenate. The real trick is to learn how to do that here and now. Our ability to stop the world and take a mental time-out several times during the day is a critical factor in health outcomes. The better we get at leaving the stress and relaxing the mind, the easier our days get and the better off we are in the long run.

I love that in Bhutan, they measure happiness. They manage spiritual and material happiness equally, and that just makes them happier. Here in the cosmopolitan world, we put way too much stock in the things we own. We are happier when we have the latest iPhone or fashion. That is not a very good way to think, and it can cause us unneeded stress and unhappiness when we can't afford those things.

Spiritually bankrupt

Here's a common complaint: "I seem to be doing everything right, such as eating the right foods, taking the right supplements and moving, yet I can't seem to get better."

If your spirit is broken and if your connection to yourself and your values has been shaken, you can become ill.

My connection to my truth and my values keeps me grounded in integrity. It helps me stay aware of who I am at the core level, understanding my individual purpose and how to be present amidst the distractions of life.

Looking back at childhood, I realise we all had something that we so badly seek as adults. We trusted our significance, we had immeasurable wonder, and we were fully present in each moment. We were overflowing with our authentic spirits.

But then we lost it. We work to become worthy, to meet other people's standards, to check off all the boxes of what's supposed to make us happy (house, job, etc.), only to realise we feel incomplete and empty. Regaining our spirit allows us to awaken to who we truly are. We all inherently want to find a deep connection with ourselves and with others, and to reclaim our purpose for being here.

Understanding that we had that so freely and naturally at one point in time is the first step to getting it back.

When spirit is not something we are able to measure on an individual level, we are able to see its qualitative impact on health in other ways.

As a Thai, I use a great example from Thai culture, which is the presence and respect of the life force within each of us and the connection between heart and mind to create the self. This idea is so ingrained in the culture.

The Thai ways correlate with psychological stress and depression in the face of perceived discrimination, local identity, race, and ethnicity. Those who practised the Thai ways had significantly lower levels of psychological stress and reduced odds for depression, over and above the effects of said sociodemographic influences.

My point here is that having a positive belief system about who we are, our place in the world, and our interactions with others means faring better against the hardest parts of life. It makes me resilient, mentally and physically.

Identifying what makes up my spirit—my attitude, values, personality, passion—helps me truly embrace my sense of self and feel greater awareness of my purpose in this life.

Breathing

Breathe in, and breathe out. Pretty simple, right? We have been doing this since the moment we came into the world, all day and every day.

We breathe 20,000 times a day. Our breathing is so ordinary, so mundane, that its true significance can easily pass us by.

I have cultivated exquisite intimacy with the breath, which, in turn, cultivates intimacy with life itself, with my body, my mind, my thoughts, my emotions, my imagination, my creativity, and beauty.

I found it is the very solid foundations of a happier and more meaningful life. It grants me the courage to accept myself with all of my faults and failings. It is a way to treat myself with the kindness, empathy, and compassion that I truly need, and it helps me to look outward and embrace the world. Spiritually speaking, the breath is where consciousness and subconscious meet. This resonated with scientific findings I came across through reading articles, examining how breathing alleviates the fear state, and also the concept that breath is the one physiological system we can control.

It is really as simple as breathing. All I need is my body, some air, and my mind—that's it. It is so simple that I can do it anywhere, any time. I use it as an inspiration for self-care and full awareness.

Breathing is the number one nutrient, as it allows oxygen to enter our body. Our bodies need it every second of the day, throughout our entire lives. I have shared with you about diet and nutrition, but oxygen is the most important nutrient we consume.

Breathing is the way we deliver oxygen to all cells in our body. If we are breathing poor quality air, we starve our muscles of oxygen. Breathing heavily through our mouth is not the best way, as it keeps the breath in the chest, which is not effective at oxygenating and removing carbon dioxide from the body. Slow, nasal, diaphragmatic breathing works well.

The following tips are what I use to remember to breathe through my nose while using my diaphragm: I practise nasal breathing deep into my belly (abdominal area), put my hand on my belly, and breathe so it can rise and fall. I visualise my breath not going into my chest, but into my diaphragm. I keep my mouth closed and my tongue at the roof of my mouth. This opens my airways and conditions the muscles to hold them open.

Once I got the hang of it, I started using this form of breathing to bring mindfulness into myself, and slowly I am mastering it to improve various missing links in my life.

I also use this technique in my fitness routine. I use it as a shortcut to a meditative state. By focusing on lengthening my exhale, I automatically increase the richness of my inhale. It is probably the easiest way to change my mental state, ground myself, and experience a deeper and more filling breath. By doing it daily, I see more results over time, just like I would with a good eating and exercise program.

Out of the 20,000 times I breathe every day, I want to have more awareness of my breathing. Whatever happens, I can't fail at breathing.

Meditation

Before I started meditating, I was typically a city person, living in the fast lane. While I loved that exciting time, it also became so incredibly stressful that I wasn't able to shake it off.

To avoid becoming spiritually bankrupt, I started meditating. It greatly helps me clear all the chaos of a busy mind, step back from my commitments, and regain balance between my mind and body. This has been an essential step in rekindling my spirit and regaining spiritual vitality. Meditation has changed my life. Meditation on a daily basis not only helps me improve my mental and spiritual health, but has also made me more focused and present so that I can fully show up for the people and causes that matter to me. For the past 15 years, I have woken up and done 20 minutes of meditation. It is an absolute staple in my life, and is as normal as brushing my teeth, but it took times to get into this habit.

Meditation has been scientifically proven to mitigate addiction, depression, anxiety, stress, and eating disorders, as well as improving cognitive function.

Meditation is a type of mental training that can increase focus and compassion for others, among a wide range of other benefits mentioned earlier. It calms me by slowing down my heart rate, my breathing, and my metabolism, all while decreasing cortisol levels, oxygen utilisation, and carbon dioxide emission.

Some of today's most successful business leaders rely on this practice to help them in their career. Oprah Winfrey, Salesforce's Marc Benioff, and Thrive Global's Arianna Huffington have all said that making meditation part of their daily routines has been key to their success.

Remember the 12 boys and their soccer coach who were trapped in a cave in Thailand for 18 days in 2018? From the video of them in the cave, it showed how calm they were, sitting there and waiting. No one was crying or anything. Stanford University meditation expert Leah Weiss, who was taught by the Dalai Lama, said that meditation was probably crucial in keeping the group alive. "For Buddhists, meditation is a go-to when distressed or in danger," Weiss told CNBC Make It. "Cognitive resources that would otherwise be hijacked by the threat can be accessed once again, meaning that problem-solving capacities increase." She went on to say, "Given that insufficient air and food was a major issue for the trapped boys, meditation is actually a very practical response to both of those concerns."

I experimented with many different meditation styles before I finally found one that resonated with me. It is a personal process.

> **"Meditation may also be thought of as a technique by which we diminish the force of old habits and develop new ones."**
> **—The Dalai Lama**

> *"If we want to save the world, we must have a plan. But no plan will work unless we meditate."*
> *—The Dalai Lama*

I have learnt from coaches, monks, and masters, and can sum up the principle of meditation as follows:

Slip into the gap. Most of the time, our mind is caught up in thoughts, emotions, and memories. Beyond this noisy internal dialogue is a state of pure awareness that is sometimes referred to as "the gap". Meditation takes us beyond the mind, and into the silence and stillness of pure consciousness. This is the ideal state in which to plant seeds of intention.

Release our intentions and desires. Once established in a state of restful awareness, release intentions and desires. The best time to plant our intentions is during the period after meditation, while our awareness remains centred in the quiet field of all possibilities. After setting an intention, let it go. Simply stop thinking about it. Continue this process for a few minutes after the meditation period each day.

Remain centred in a state of restful awareness. Interaction is much more powerful when it comes from a place of contentment than if it arises from a sense of lack or need. Stay centred, and refuse to be influenced by other people's doubts or criticisms. Our higher self knows that everything is alright and will be alright, even without knowing the timing or the details of what will happen.

Detach from the outcome. Relinquish any rigid attachment to a specific result, and live in the wisdom of uncertainty. Attachment is based on fear and insecurity, while detachment is based on the unquestioning belief in the power of our true self. Intend for everything to work out as it should, then let go and allow opportunities and openings to come our way.

Let the universe handle the details. Our focused intentions set the infinite organising power of the universe in motion. Trust that infinite organising power to orchestrate the complete fulfilment of your desires. Don't listen to the voice that says that you have to be in charge or that obsessive vigilance is the only way to get anything done. The outcome that you'll try so hard to force may not be as good for you as the one that comes naturally. Release your intentions into the fertile ground of pure potential, and they will bloom when the season is right.

When I first started, my teacher gave me an ancient Sanskrit word that I repeat silently in my head over and over again while sitting upright or walking silently. It is called a *mantra*, and it basically acts as a tool to guide me into a relaxed state of mind. No one's brain can repeat the same word over and over (in my case, for 20 minutes straight) without having other thoughts, so my mind drifts, which is part of the process and is totally normal! I just let those thoughts come, and once I realise I have trailed off from the mantra, I start repeating it again. Once 20 minutes is complete, I have a two- to three-minute "come down" from the meditation, which is where I say what I am thankful for and just give myself positive affirmations. This allows me to not be dizzy/light-headed after the deep state of relaxation I just put my brain in!

I meditate right after waking up, and start my day by drinking a big glass of warm water. I go to a place where I can be alone and settle in a space of sacred silence. I use Navy SEAL box breathing, which is a practice of deep diaphragmatic breathing meant to be done in a quiet and controlled setting. To put it simply, I inhale for a count of five to seven, hold for a count of five to seven, exhale for five to seven, and hold my breath again for a count of five to seven. I then take a few minutes to reflect. I think about who I am and my personal ethos, and establish positive thoughts through gratitude. I reflect on things like the following:

- Seeing myself for what I am, a piece of consciousness directly connected to every other life.

- What and for whom I am grateful. I bring to mind big or small things that I am truly grateful for. I express gratitude for those things and feel this gratitude vibrate all throughout my body.

- Forgiveness to those with whom I have had conflict. I imagine that person in front of me and apologise for any wrong that I brought to them. I ask for forgiveness. I forgive them for any wrong that they brought to me. I feel that sense of forgiveness all throughout my body.

- Daily intention: who can I reach out to and serve or thank today? I visualise myself living the best version for today, I make it as vivid as possible with emotions of joy, excitement, and gratitude. The purpose is to visualise myself making an amazingly wonderful day. This prepares my mind with purpose and winning.

- My perfect future: what is my purpose? I mentally tell myself all the different aspects of my life as I want them to unfold for a better life.

- Blessing: I call on my inner straight and higher power that I believe in and ask for energy, support, and blessings to make my dreams/purposes come through. I feel this support and energy all around me with positive/protective energy embracing me.

When that is completed, I slowly come out of meditation by counting backwards from ten to one.

This simple ritual is designed to fit into as little as 20 minutes as part of my first hour of the day.

The next 40 minutes of my first hour of the day are dedicated to movement and learning. Sweating first thing in the morning helps release brain-derived neurotrophic factor (BDNF), which helps repair brain cells damaged by stress.

I split my learning portion into two key areas: personal mastery and professional education. In this portion, I can listen to a podcast, read a book, review my study notes, etc. This habit of learning more enables me to do more and better. I feel life is more meaningful when I spend it as an eternal student. Top performers have one thing in common: they persist in learning. I feed my mind and keep myself on top of things. I read, listen, and watch. I always take in newer ideas so that I will never find myself facing a wall. Sometimes, the reason we can't break through is because we don't know how.

I adapted the above from Robin Sharma's coaching, and it is really working well for me. It has four awakenings: 1) enrich my mind, 2) nurture my emotional life, 3) feed my physical life, 4) tend to my soul.

By getting up an hour earlier, I have extra time to replenish and refuel my body, mind, and soul. It helps me to realise that how I begin my day is how I live my day. By establishing a fulfilling morning routine, I benefit mentally, physically, and even spiritually. A morning routine means being in control of my day instead of my day controlling me.

Once I have specific routines in place, I can go on autopilot for these healthy activities, and eventually even add new positive habits that give me confidence and good input to start my day.

In other words, if I can get the morning to go my way, the rest of the day will be smooth sailing. So I make myself a first-rate morning routine. As a matter of fact, practice makes perfect. It took me a while to stick with it. For you, consider starting with some healthy habits during your morning routine, like not looking at your phone as soon as you wake up. It just might leak over into other areas of your life, too.

Gratitude

Gratitude is a powerful force that we can use to expand our happiness, create loving relationships, and even improve our health.

Many scientific studies, including research by renowned psychologists Robert Emmons and Michael E. McCullough, have found that people who consciously focus on gratitude experience greater emotional wellbeing and physical health than those who don't.

From that, I understood that if I wanted more happiness, joy, and energy, then gratitude was clearly a crucial quality to cultivate. It is a fullness of heart that moves us from limitation and fear to expansion and love. When we are appreciating something, our ego moves out of the way, and we connect with our soul. Gratitude brings our attention into the present, which is the only place where miracles can unfold. The deeper our appreciation, the more we see with the eyes of the soul, and the more our life flows in harmony with the creative power of the universe.

FEELGOODX
8-PHASE MEDITATION

Daily meditation is a life-changing experience.

Choose a calming environment, sit in a comfortable position, close your eyes, and take deep breath. With gentle relaxation of your physical body, move your focus to your body, part by part, and relax each section as you go.

01 NAVY SEAL BOX BREATHING TECHNIQUE

Inhale for a count of five, hold for a count of five, exhale for five, and hold for five. I count to about 60 before moving to the next step.

02 REFLECT ON WHO I AM, MY PERSONAL ETHOS

A key element is authenticity. Knowing who I am, where I stand on morality, and why I stand there is an essential step toward making better choices.

03 CONSCIOUSNESS

See myself for what I am, a piece of consciousness directly connected to every other life.

04 WHAT AND FOR WHOM AM I GRATEFUL?

Bring to mind big or small things or people I am truly grateful for. Express gratitude for those things and feel this gratitude vibrate all throughout my body.

05 FORGIVENESS

Who have I had conflict with? Imagine that person in front of me and apologise for any wrong that I brought to them. Ask for forgiveness. Forgive any wrong that they brought to me. Feel the feeling of forgiveness all throughout my body.

06 DAILY INTENTIONS

Who can I reach out to and serve or think about today? I visualise myself living the best version of today. I make it as vivid as possible in emotions of joy, excitement, and gratitude. This prepares my mind with purpose and a winning mentality.

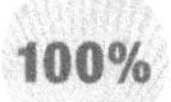

07 MY PERFECT FUTURE

What is my purpose? I mentally tell myself all the different aspects of my life as I want them to unfold for a better life.

08 BLESSINGS

I call on my inner strength and higher power that I believe in and ask for energy, support, and blessings to make my dreams/purposes come through. Feel this support and energy all around me with positive/protective energy embracing me.

Bring myself slowly out of meditation within 2-3 minutes.

I like to make gratitude lists for the simple things making me happy right now. The daily grind can make me overlook all the things in my life that make me feel happy and fulfilled. I get so hung up on what's gone wrong that day that I can easily forget about the simple things that make my life enjoyable. Expressing gratitude for the good things that surround me can help me to de-stress, savour each moment, and be thankful for what I have. This is my gratitude list:

Reading and listening. I used to have a tendency to dive straight into work after waking up, which is not the healthiest of habits. I was giving myself zero time to wake up and enjoy the new day. I decided to change my first hour of the day and also the last hour before sleeping. Part of the time is for reading and listening. I feel happier, and my work has been better and more productive.

Whenever, I read or work, I use time management Pomodoros. I downloaded an app which can set the timer to 25 minutes and focus for that time. When the time is right, take five minutes off. Each 25-minute chunk is a Pomodoro. I take five minutes off each time until my task is done.

This technique was invented in 1987 by Francesco Cirillo to boost productivity. It is named after the tomato-shaped kitchen timer that he used to help him study at university.

Travel. Whether it is a holiday abroad or a weekend away near home, travel is something that never fails to ignite my inspiration and creativity. Spending time with family and friends is super important to me, and travelling to see them is something I do regularly with my wife. It does not matter if it is travelling to a local park, across the country, or to another country. Travel is something that makes me incredibly happy, and I am very privileged to be able to do it a few times a year.

According to new research, there is an important connection between taking time off and living longer. According to the findings, the longer one holiday, the more longevity improves. In the study, those who holidayed for three weeks or more each year lived longer than those who holidayed for three weeks or less.

Gratitude journal. Since ancient times, philosophers and sages from every spiritual tradition have taught that cultivating gratitude is key to experiencing deeper levels of happiness, fulfilment, and wellbeing.

I reclaimed my life by journalling. It helped me accept myself and fix the habits that were holding me back. I have gotten a lot of my practice because I have a clear focus going into each session. I am reflecting on the thoughts and habits that made up my day so that I can see where I am going right and where I can improve. I am celebrating my victories, and I am accepting and encouraging myself in the areas where I have faltered. I am looking for insights and clues to things that I can change (or do better) to be the very best version of me.

I don't dwell on negativity. If I have an effusion of negative thoughts that wrecked my day, I don't have to relive every single thought and bring myself back to that dark cloud. Instead, I write down simply that I had negative thoughts. I stopped the negativity with affirmations or something else, and wrote how I prevailed. I congratulate myself, then move on to the other details of my day. Negativity happens to everyone, and it is how we respond to it that counts.

Sometimes I have crappy days, but my journalling habit and positive attitude make those days rare. And whenever they do happen, there is always a culprit. As I journal, I find the culprit and come up with the solution.

Nine times out of ten, my bad days are caused by a lack of mindfulness. I know that I could have done better, but for some reason, I got hung up on little things. So, I identify those little things and plan against them.

It is hard to be grateful sometimes, especially when I am feeling down. But the option to be grateful is always there and always important. I journal with an attitude of gratitude. I search out the things and people and events and efforts that made me feel really grateful.

I find a ton of gratitude in the little moments when I made good decisions, even when it was hard. I express gratitude when I do something that makes me feel mature and good.

When I focus on small decisions with an attitude of gratitude, I will make even better decisions, which will make me even more grateful. It is the beginning of an amazing positive feedback loop, and it has changed my life. It all started with the decision to be grateful.

Lastly, together with the first step, I find my focus. I write down the date. I immediately write a couple of lines about what I am.

I always start with the affirmation because they super-charge my focus and eliminate the chance of lingering on negativity.

At the end of my journalling session, I focus on applauding myself for the incredible job I did. I focus on hope for an even better tomorrow. I can always have a better day tomorrow, no matter how good or incredibly bad today was.

What I learn from journalling is to focus on improving my practice. Those better days can and will be every day.

Creativity

> **"Art is never finished, only abandoned."**
> **—Leonardo da Vinci**

I may not be an artist or designer, but the truth is everyone is creative. It is impossible not to be. We use our minds every day to create things—ideas, products, solutions, and responses. Being creative is a part of being human. When we express ourselves, we are able to honour our creative selves.

Creativity is not always painting, photography, writing, or art. It can be updating my bucket list, reading an article that inspires me and applying the lessons, or researching new ways to solve old problems.

Creativity means that I am creating. I can change the way I think and act, questioning assumptions or building relationships. I can come up with new solutions to problems, develop new ideas, or reinterpret existing ideas. Being creative is essential to overcoming obstacles and being resilient. Creativity helps me navigate life, and creative expression keeps me happy and healthy.

Some people are more creative than others simply because they have practised it. The truth, though, is that we are all creative; we just express it in different ways.

Creativity is a practice and process, never an end result. The more I can enjoy the process as a journey instead of reaching a destination, the more I find the output to be more passionate, fulfilling, and unique.

Creativity is the ability to transcend traditional ideas, rules, and patterns to craft my own unique interpretation of the world around me. We are all naturally creative to some extent—maybe we show it through our clothing or hairstyle. At one point, I was into photography with the idea that "a picture speaks a thousand words." As often as I could, I took pictures of what inspired me. This exercise helped me see the beauty in everyday life, whether it was family and friends, a delicious meal, the sunset, or a street scene in Bangkok.

Music

When I focus on self-care, I make sure to eat nutritious foods, exercise regularly, meditate, and get enough sleep. These are the basic building blocks of self-care, after all. I also find that music is a powerful force for healing and an improved sense of wellbeing.

Music gives me positive feelings, especially if it's a favourite song. When I am upset, it helps to put together a sad playlist. It gives me a feeling of wonder, peace, power, and nostalgia while listening to melancholy tunes. I also think music may increase immune functioning. When I was seriously ill, my wife turned on relaxing nature sounds and calm music for me, and I found that it helped in my recovery. There is even research in this area recently that levels of IgA (an antibody in our immune system) showed a greater increase after listening to music, as compared to those who listened to a clicking sound or silence, or even a radio broadcast. All the more reason to make some time for music on a daily basis.

It is easy to make music a part of your daily life, like while exercising, taking a morning walk or run, or stretching. For me, music helps to shift my internal state of stress. Instead of being frustrated when I encounter traffic jams, I sing in the car.

Singing takes the positive effects of listening to music to another level. Singing is one of the best ways to shift the vibrations of my thoughts. It helps me to slow and regulate my breathing and promotes relaxation. Singing in the shower or in the car with the songs I know helps me be in a better mood, inspires me, and helps me relax. Just try and pay attention to how different you feel after a few minutes of singing aloud, and make note of the songs that make you feel best so you can put them on repeat when you need them.

Many of my friends and colleagues love karaoke. It helps relieve stress and boosts self-esteem and confidence, while also building social connections, which are all major life extenders. Plus, it helps build bonds and banish conflict. Of Japanese origin, karaoke has come a long way since its inception in the early 70s. The best part: it is more about having fun than about singing really well, and anyone can do it. It has become a social phenomenon in Asian countries and is one of the healthiest forms of entertainment. Some studies have shown that singing can even surpass the effects of yoga on your heart rate, breathing, and general wellbeing.

Music makes people happy, not only when they listen to it, but also when they sing. Numerous studies suggest singing is the best therapy for being happy.

FEELGOODX

LIVE YOUR LIFE, LOVE YOUR LIFE

Relationships

———

> *"The most important relationship in your life is the relationship you have with yourself. Because no matter what happens, you will always be with yourself."*
> *—Diane Von Fürstenberg*

Louis Cozolino, professor of psychology at Pepperdine University, emphasises the positive impact of human relationships on our health and longevity:

"Of all the experiences we need to survive and thrive, it is the experience of relating to others that is the most meaningful and important," he writes. "Our brains are social organs, and that means we are wired to connect with each other and to interact in groups. A life that maximises social interaction and human-to-human contact is good for the brain at every stage, particularly the aging brain."

The well-known, long-running Harvard Medical School Nurses' Health Study was one of the early studies to reveal how being socially integrated can lead to greater health, life satisfaction, and longevity over time.

In a study of elderly Hong Kong residents, researchers found that those who spent more time cultivating social relationships had a significant drop in cortisol levels during the day, which could explain why positive relationships help us learn better, stay healthier, and live longer.

Best-selling author Dan Buettner published a cover story for *National Geographic* titled "The Secret of Living Longer," which highlighted areas around the world dubbed Blue Zones. He noticed common patterns among the people in these Blue Zones, even though they are far from one another. These include strong family connections and strong social connections, in addition to an absence of smoking, daily physical activity centred on walking, and a plant-heavy diet with very few animal proteins.

Many Blue Zones emphasise family and community, but bonding reaches its peak in Okinawa, Japan. Okinawans are supported by their *moai*, a small but tightknit social circle meant to be there through all of life's ups and downs, which provides sufficient social support to dull mental stressors and reinforces shared healthy behaviours.

Today, the idea of *moai* has expanded to become more of a social support network, a cultural tradition for built-in companionship. In small neighbourhoods across Okinawa, friends meet for a common purpose—sometimes daily and sometimes a couple of days a week—to gossip, experience life, and share advice and even financial assistance when needed.

The human brain is almost endlessly adaptive throughout its life cycle, and change is as possible for older people as for infants. As we grow older, what is lost in quick recall and short-term memory is balanced by an ability to reflect on and hold multiple perspectives.

Various studies show that many healthy older adults show no significant brain volume loss past 100 years of age if they have maintained close ties to others. They tend to be more extroverted and have higher morals. They reach out to others, give and receive support, and maintain attachments.

My idea of *moai* is having a few friends who I have kept in contact with since my school days. It has been more than 30 years, and we are still in contact, and we help each other without any conditions. Apart from family, this is my closest inner circle. I find that it is better to have a small number of tight, meaningful relationships; this is one of the highest predictors of happiness.

When it comes to relationships, I love Arianna Huffington's three steps to add more virtue by becoming "go givers."

1. Make a personal connection with someone you would not normally connect with.

2. Give small kindnesses throughout the day.

3. Focus on all you are grateful for. Pope Francis once said, "Gratitude is a flower that blooms in noble souls."

When I focus on becoming a "go giver," I feel like bringing light into the world. As life becomes lighter, I open a channel for the light to enter me. This is the light of awareness, freedom, truth, and love. The greatest influence we can possibly have is to radiate our own being from the level of the true self. It is not out of duty I let my light shine, but rather out of joy to bring light into the world.

> **"Let your presence light new light in the hearts of others."**
> **—Mother Teresa**

The mindset of "go giver" is joy, kindness, and politeness. Choose to say things with a smile, and say more pleasant words.

Smiling is the first element that I learnt from the book *How to Win Friends and Influence People* by Dale Carnegie. It is our actions, not our words, that show others what we think of them. Thus, when meeting someone new, the easiest way to say, "I like you and I am happy to meet you" is with a smile.

We humans are suckers for people who smile at us. If we meet someone new and see them smile, we tend to automatically like them as well. The smile of a baby, for example, immediately makes us feel warm and fuzzy inside, as does seeing a dog wag his tail like crazy because he is happy to see us.

From the same book, I also learned that if you want good relationships, don't criticise! Criticising someone is easy, but it takes character to be understanding and to forgive others for their mistakes and shortcomings. If I want others to like me, I have to try to understand what drives them, accept their shortcomings, and make it a rule to never criticise them openly, for this criticism will only come back to harm me.

Many successful individuals have actually made it a habit to never openly criticise others. Benjamin Franklin, for instance, claimed that the secret of his success was to "speak ill of no man."

Actually, the Asean way of communicating is very indirect and far less verbose than what the English-speaking west is familiar with. In order to maintain harmony throughout a conversation and prevent loss of face on the other end, we may use ambiguous speech and understatements to convey a message in a more subtle way.

I show appreciation and make myself someone people enjoy being with by using simple phrases such as, "Thank you," and "I am sorry." I have also learned to give sincere praise. Our appreciation must be honest, as people can see through phony flattery.

In addition, I give my full attention to the other person. I make a conscious effort to show that I am genuinely interested in everything they have to say.

Sigmund Freud was famous for his listening skills. He excelled at showing others how very interesting he found everything they said, and, in return, they felt completely comfortable talking to him and would reveal even their most private emotions and experiences.

I love the Japanese culture of nodding. Japanese people often nod to acknowledge what is said. This does not always mean they agree or understand; it is primarily a polite gesture to show that they are into the conversation.

Whenever I meet someone, I find something I admire about them and tell them about it. Regardless of who I meet, my mission is to find something to admire in them. The easiest way to get into the mindset of appreciating others is to keep in mind the golden rule: treat others as you would like others to treat you.

If I want to win others over, I show them my full appreciation and I am enthusiastic about it. I used to be terrible at remembering names. I make an effort now to remember the names of those I meet, and I try to use their name as we talk.

Another area of weakness for me was avoiding all arguments. I have learned to be thankful for the other person's input and to think about their reasoning instead of automatically arguing to bolster my views. I avoid arguments except when they are absolutely necessary and inevitable, and I keep my emotions out of them.

Recognise that we all make mistakes. Whenever I do, I admit my mistake quickly and clearly.

Do you know Bruce Lee? He was a Hong Kong-American actor, director, martial artist, martial arts instructor, and philosopher. When I was young, Bruce Lee had an impact on me as an Asian from his hero roles in his movies. To my surprise, combing through Bruce Lee quotes many years later, I found his wisdom could also improve my relationships. Consider this quote: "Empty your mind; be formless, shapeless—like water. Now, you put water into a cup, it becomes the cup, you put water into a bottle, it becomes the bottle, you put it in a teapot. Now water can flow, or it can crash. Be water, my friend."

This really gave me a reminder to be like water making my way through cracks. Do not be assertive, but adjust to the situation, and I shall find a way around or through it. If nothing within me stays rigid, outward things will disclose themselves. One more quote from him to remind me to be authentic is this one: "Always be yourself, have faith in yourself, do not go out and look for a successful personality and duplicate it."

This quote reminds me of Akira Kurosawa, a Japanese master who made great films. Steven Spielberg called him "the pictorial Shakespeare of our time." Despite being held up by those outside Japan as the foremost exporter of Japanese cinema, Kurosawa was decried as too western by detractors at home. Yet, he still made his work with local theatrical tradition, and was probably the greatest filmmaker in the samurai genre. He once said that he found a western-looking format most practical, but that he really only made his pictures for young Japanese in their 20s.

The quote from Bruce Lee and the way Kurosawa thought gave me the confidence to be myself and made me feel proud to be Asian. Most importantly, they taught me what it means to be human—about how messy, complex, and ultimately irrational I can be. Many times, I am driven by emotions and passions as much as I am by reason; I employ mythical imagination as much as argumentative thinking. From Kurosawa's films, I have learned many useful things like human warmth, social urgency, and a way of speaking directly to the human heart. Of course, all these are only movies, but it is so much fun thinking around the notion that truth is a human fabrication, and that everything can be endlessly constructed and deconstructed. It is up to humans like us.

To really achieve all those behaviours that I mentioned, my very first step is to change my relationship with mobile gadgets. It was very difficult at first to accept disconnection, staying present in my everyday moments and truly embracing myself and my passions. I realise that I can refresh, reconnect, and tune in to myself every day simply by unplugging in small ways. Here's how I do it:

- I maintain a tech-free bedroom and also have no phone at the dinner table

- Tech fasting. I refrain from checking Instagram, Facebook, LinkedIn, and communication apps like LINE most of the time to stay present in my in-person life.

- I track how much time I spend on my phone using the Moment app.

- I put it away while I work and only check it during break times.

I have found that disconnecting daily, even if just for these micro-moments, makes such a huge difference in my mood and brings me back to that place of unrelenting peace and creativity. Most importantly, it improves and makes a big difference in my relationships.

Another point that is important to acknowledge in relationships is that men and women tend to think of the world in different ways, with men looking closely to separate and categorise things, and women stepping back to see patterns and connections. The best minds will have ready access to both ways of thinking. We attain masculinity and femininity both from our genes and our upbringing, so it's best to embrace this duality within us to improve relationships and make us more empathetic to the opposite sex. It can also improve problem-solving, creativity, and confidence.

In Asia, unlike in the west, a lot of business people are not accustomed to "business only" relationships. Rather, we prefer to create a friendly and personal relationship first, and then conduct business later, and, aside from cultural preference, there is a strong business reason to do so. Despite the fact that almost every company will sign a contract at the beginning of a business deal, the actual ability of a company to enforce said contract is low, especially for small companies. A lot of countries in Asia have ineffective legal systems and can take years to successfully resolve cases. Many firms don't have the time or money to wait for a favourable resolution. By focusing on developing a strong relationship first, as opposed to a formal and tightly worded contract, Asean businesspeople rely on strong relationships to be assured of a long-term and profitable collaboration.

In the words of Sun Tzu, the Chinese military strategist who wrote a book called *The Art of War* some 2,500 years ago, "Build your enemies a golden bridge." This means we have to always find a mutually satisfactory solution by bridging the gap between their interests and ours. It is also important to help the other save face and make the outcome look like victory for them.

The word for this is *guanxi* in Chinese, or the phrase, "It is not what you know, but who you know." This idea takes on a much greater significance in Asia, in which business organisations and social circles are often nepotistic in nature. That is, relationships do not merely supplement an individual's effectiveness in business and dealings in everyday life; instead, relationships form the foundations upon which business and society are built.

Actually, I believe this culture came from a 2,000-year-old Chinese philosophy, Confucianism, which places a strong emphasis on proper relationships being the key to social harmony.

As mentioned, in Asia we place a strong emphasis on building and maintaining networks of personal and business relationships. Beyond the importance of relationship networks, I've also heard the word *yuanfen* from my wife. Though this is a somewhat ambiguous term, many Chinese people come to believe that some relationships contain a touch of destiny, and, as a result, this can lead to even greater commitment with regards to certain relationships.

I understand *yuan* by itself to mean karma or fate; *fen* can mean the division between two halves. When combined together, *yuanfen* can be defined as a fate or chance that brings two or more people together, or a predestined affinity.

I think a large part of the significance of *yuanfen* draws upon an idea inherent in the Buddhist faith that has long been prevalent in Chinese culture. Practitioners of Buddhism believe that all living things are reincarnated at the end of their lives. By itself, the probability of two people coming together is low. Two individuals might go through countless incarnations on Earth before finally finding each other, which would make such a meeting (and relationship) even more special and profound.

I take *yuanfen* as a potential to influence and affect the formation of important personal and business relationships. But there is not really a reliable method to determine whether there is truly an innate connection between two people. The Chinese chiefly rely on common background, interests, and emotional impressions to let them know whether they have *yuanfen* with a specific person. For example, if two people working in the big city meet and, upon conversing, discover that they are from the same small town, they might feel as if they have *yuanfen*. This would be especially true if they met by chance on multiple occasions.

Learning lessons from eastern martial arts

Thanks to movies like *The Karate Kid*, the art of karate is almost synonymous with martial arts. In reality, karate is only a small part of the martial arts and represents only one aspect of the Japanese arts. Actually, Asia is home to many different martial arts, including the many kung fu styles of China, but the martial arts of Korea are probably the most similar to their Japanese counterparts.

As in the Japanese martial arts of judo, jujitsu and aikido, you need to avoid pitting your strength directly against your opponent's. Since breaking down the other side's resistance usually only increases it, you try to go around their resistance. That is the way to break through. Breakthroughs in relationship or negotiations are the opposite of imposing our position on the other side. Rather than telling them what to do, we let them figure it out. Rather than pressuring them to change their mind, we create an environment in which they can break through their own resistance: we only need to help them.

Asian culture puts a strong emphasis on being in harmony with the universe. That is why it is difficult for a western mind to understand the concept of "learning martial arts so you don't have to use them." Martial arts put emphasis on meeting hardness with softness. The eastern mind makes no distinction between the self and the universe. Moreover, in the past, martial arts were a part of life, not a sport. Students learned to be humble, pay respect to their elders (ancestors), and honour their schools or families. In modern times, we can call on the virtues of warrior in our relationships, including rectitude, courage, benevolence, politeness/propriety, honesty/sincerity and loyalty.

There are also three states of mind, including *zanshin* (awareness, alertness, preparedness), *mushin* (no or clear mind), and *fudōshin* (emotional balance). *Zanshin* requires that we are always alert enough to accurately assess our surroundings.

Mushin is a key theme among the ninja, but for us, it is the ability to clear the mind of all techniques, to flow with the opponent's movement, and to create. *Fudŏshin* is the emotional balance we all endeavour to reach.

These concepts are not particularly difficult to understand, but to achieve them together in harmony is a skill in and of itself. However, these are the foundations on which we can build our relationships with ourselves and others, build our strength of body and mind, and govern our mental, spiritual, and emotional wellbeing.

The key is to show interest with sincerity and be more of a giver than a taker.

When it comes to relationships, I really admire Khun Nirun, my former colleague in Bangkok who is a real giver and is willing to share his story:

"When talking about relationships, I always think of my mother who taught me and was my role model. She was a great person who was always kind to everybody.

I learn a lot from my relationships. Various relationships have taught me some core concepts, including happy life, gratitude, sincerity, learning, and innovation.

Happy Life: work hard, play hard, enjoy everyone I meet. No drama. If someone shares with me in a negative way, I always listen, but the way I advise my colleagues is to think of the future and be positive.

Gratitude: I learn from the strengths of influential people in my life to adapt my character. I always respect them and am grateful for them.

Sincerity: It must be from the heart. Sincerity is not to say everything you think, but to mean everything you say and act trustworthy.

Learning: I learn from everyone's experiences, and from how people achieve their goals.

Innovation: Innovative thought can help me become effective and efficient.

I come from a poor farming family, but I have had the chance to meet good people. I set a goal every year for what I plan to achieve, and relationships are part of my success. Never give up on a challenging situation, and be patient. Learn from a mistake.

I love to give to and share with family, colleagues, old friends, and others. I am happy to see their success."

Vulnerability

> **"Vulnerability sounds like truth and feels like courage. Truth and courage are not always comfortable, but they are never weakness."**
> **—Brené Brown**

These days, vulnerability is about as popular a buzz word as mindfulness, thanks to the incredible work of Brené Brown, who said, "vulnerability is not about fear and grief and disappointment. It is the birthplace of everything we are hungry for." Her books have opened up an entirely new vocabulary around the best way to live our lives authentically.

When I was young, I thought being a man meant being tough, being strong, being macho. Rarely did I hear anything about being kind, caring, or vulnerable.

Vulnerability has gotten a bad rap. The idea has been perpetuated that vulnerability is weakness, so men feel the need to put up a front.

Lately, I discovered that vulnerability is nothing like what I have been taught. Vulnerability seems to be one of the keys to having everything I have ever wanted. It is authentic. It is inviting. It is attractive. Vulnerability is sexy.

Vulnerability is the willingness to have and be all of me. In vulnerability, I stop pretending, I come out of hiding, and I start to choose what actually works for me instead of trying to live up to other people's opinions.

When I choose to be vulnerable with the people in my life, things start to change. The things that I have been seeking, the things I desire, start to show up. Why? It is simple, really. Vulnerability is about me being me. Vulnerability is about dropping all barriers. When I choose vulnerability rather than trying to force things to happen, the things I desire easily come to me.

As I open myself to vulnerability, I begin to choose trust rather than wait for someone to earn it. It becomes a gift I give to myself. I was very guarded and kept myself carefully protected with the myth that I wouldn't get hurt that way. Yet the hurt is there, no matter how many layers I have over my heart. Whether or not I choose to feel it, and whether or not it is in my conscious mind, it is in my energy, and I am informed by it. Vulnerability allows me to feel when I am hurt. It does not open me up for more. When I feel vulnerable, I can work with my vulnerability, and when we work with it, the hurt usually informs me, and I can move on with the wisdom I have received. I become trusting of myself and my ability to heal, instead of expecting that other people will behave in a way I consider acceptable. This is the beginning of letting go of needing others' behaviour to bring us healing.

Finally, I love these two quotes from Brené Brown, which give me a clear direction on how I should live and behave:

"Authenticity is a collection of choices that we have to make every day. It is about the choice to show up and be real. The choice to be honest. The choice to let our true selves be seen."

"You are imperfect and you are wired for struggle, but you are worthy of love and belonging."

FEELGOODX
LIVE YOUR LIFE, LOVE YOUR LIFE

Your journey begins now!

> *"A journey of a thousand miles begins with a single step."*
> *—Lao Tzu*

Right now, discontent runs rampant in our daily life: it pops up on social feeds, lurks in conversations, and spouts from every talking head in the media. But discontent only thrives when we let ourselves feel helpless. You are not helpless. You have it within your power to create meaningful change in your life.

Every day, we have infinite opportunities to make our relationships, careers, and communities just a bit better. To make thoughtful, intentioned decisions, followed by determination.

There is one thing you can do to improve all areas of your life at the same time: invest in yourself. The most famous investor of all time, Warren Buffett, says, "The best investment you can make is in yourself."

Our lives are made up or moments stacked one on top of the other. Some are small, offering you the opportunity to make little shifts toward your goals. In other moments, you are afforded the chance to make monumental shifts—powerful shifts which will have ripple effects for years to come.

It is time to radically shift your life toward the good. It is time to find gifts in adversity. It is time to create lasting change in your life.

> **"Whatever the mind of man can conceive and believe, it can achieve."**
> **—Napoleon Hill**

How? Here are my suggestions for your journey to bring FeelGoodX into your life:

- Consider a whole bunch of options. Before you double down on something, consider a whole lot of things. Find something that really captures your imagination.

> **"Passion is energy. Feel the power that comes from focusing on what excites you."**
> **—Oprah Winfrey**

Here is my formula:

1. Encounter a lot of options and find the thing that really interests you

2. By engaging with that option, see if it turns from an interest into a fascination. If it doesn't, move on to something else.

3. Turn the fascination into a full-blown passion by going down the path of gaining mastery. Give yourself over to it completely. Go all in. In the process of gaining mastery and really becoming great at it, you will either determine it is

your passion, or you will get sick of it and move on until you hit on the thing that really sticks.

4. Demand greatness of yourself. If you want to have the kind of drive to see things through, you are going to have to become the kind of person who sees things through. It is that simple.

To do that, tell yourself and anyone who will listen that you are the type of person who strives for greatness every day and does not stop until it's been achieved. At first, you are going to feel like a fraud saying it because it's not yet true. But repeating that to yourself and to others will make it come true.

So, start demanding greatness of yourself today. It is the only way to start building the fire within yourself because the fire itself will require constant stoking. If it is not part of your identity to stoke that fire, to actually force your dreams into becoming reality, you will never achieve escape velocity over your "wants" and make them true "needs."

- Obsess over the utility of your skills. It is important to understand that skills are meaningful because they let you do things that others can't. Like sport, the idea is to get so good that you can win against someone who has trained their whole life to beat you. When you get that good, you are literally unstoppable because people actually can't stop you.

You have a superior skill set and you are now so good that people truly can't ignore you. This translates to having the "real" need because you know you can actually make your dreams come true.

Dreams are daunting and create laziness when you don't believe you can actually make them come true. But when you know that your efforts will be rewarded with success, suddenly you want to stare at your dreams all day and carefully plan out and then carry out your plans. It all feels real because you are capable of delivering real results. This one is key! When you know you have built your skills up to the point that on your best day you can beat anyone, suddenly playing the game will become your obsession.

- Accept that you, you, you can change the world. When you have developed your skills and gotten so good that you can execute your dream, suddenly you'll realise that you can change the world around you, literally.

When you develop your skills, you stop feeling powerless and you start feeling like you can do whatever you set your mind to. When you feel like that and you set your mind to something that you are really passionate about and you think will change the world for the better, suddenly the thought of making your dreams a reality becomes intoxicating. It starts to consume your thoughts, and then your actions.

And at that point you want to start shifting into a need. You want it so badly you can taste it. It is so close—only a matter of execution. And now, you are not going to let anything stop you. That is how it begins.

- Take pride in working on the jigsaw puzzle longer than anyone else. It is not going to be easy. You are going to have to go after it hard. You are going to slip or even fall. But if you can keep after it long after it has stopped being fun, long after everyone else has given up, you will actually solve the puzzle of execution and get to the other side, where you have made your dream a reality. But it will ultimately come down to perseverance.

- A winning vs. losing mentality. You need things that feed your fire to sustain you over time, and winning is one of them. But you have got to teach yourself to absolutely love competing and winning.

Feel the joy of victory, the gratitude of being able to play the game, and the pride that comes with having faced your inadequacies one by one while continuing to learn and grow as a human. When you have a strong "why" and what you are doing is helping others, winning isn't selfish—it is about moving one step closer to doing something beautiful for the world.

You need to hate losing. You must hate the thought of that so much that you are willing to keep pushing, learning from every failure until you get the ultimate victory.

> **"Failure is not fatal, but failing to change might be."**
> **—John Wooden**

- Tell people what you are going to accomplish. As you are trying to do something beautiful for yourself and the world, your vision will excite other people. The more they get excited and offer to help, the more obligated you will feel to see it through.

Start now, and stack each of those things on top of each other. You will come out the other side with enough internal motivation to see anything through.

> **"It doesn't matter how slowly you go as long as you do not stop."**
> **—Confucius**

I hope you do. With that, we will live in a world where a whole new bunch of hungry people are out there making it a better place by executing their beautiful dreams.

FEELGOODX

LIVE YOUR LIFE, LOVE YOUR LIFE

Final words

> *"How many cares one loses when one decides not to be something but to be someone."*
> *—Coco Chanel*

Every day our lives are shaped by forces we may not even realise are part of us. Some of the most prevalent themes that get reinforced in society are winner and loser, lovable and unlovable, victim and perpetrator, beautiful and ugly, powerful and powerless. When we put ourselves in one of these mental boxes, we lose the power to shape our own story.

For me, I define myself by choosing who I want to be.

As life becomes richer and more fulfilling, my entire perspective shifts. I see that life itself, the simple fact of being here, is cause for celebration. I celebrate that the true self brings constant love and support. I recognise the spiritual core of every human being is freedom, love, and joy. In a world weighed down by many burdens, this is the most uplifting truth I can follow.

Every day, I accept the incredible gift of being here, and I look for at least one thing to celebrate.

After all, the transformation is about my personal story. We write our life story by the choices we make. We are all living a personal story, and every story has ups and downs, low points and high points. But what is important is the theme that structures and guides our story.

When my story has had positive, life-supporting themes, I have found the key to transformation. I discovered that changing my theme is more effective than trying to fix myself one issue at a time. The most positive themes include lightness, worthiness, self-acceptance, evolution, and love.

Your theme should be aimed at making you FeelGoodX every day. It should open new possibilities. It should give you optimism that you are being renewed.

Together, let us create a FeelGoodX tribe with a common cause for freely accessible, community-created information that can help us succeed in the mission to always feel good. We'll be a tribe that shares values and ideas as our own. With the reach of internet and especially social media, geography is no longer a barrier to growth. The goal is to create real sustainable growth, starting from our values. Let's tell our friends to join this movement. We will use feelgoodx.com to share knowledge and organise projects, and we'll use Facebook, YouTube, and Instagram to share updates about developments.

Don't let what we have been previously conditioned to believe stop us from this movement. What we need in the world are more heretics: people who question the status quo and the existing dogmas and take action without hesitation. The media primes us with a story about heretics, filled with self-delusion or inevitable downfalls. We can overcome this false narrative together by talking ourselves out of the fear, reminding ourselves that everything worth doing is risky, and that the world needs and demands the change we are trying to make. Fear is what is stopping us from changing the status quo. But together and with today's technology, there are no excuses anymore not to live our life and love our life. We can do this together, and we can start by being part of the FeelGoodX community.

Lastly, let me share a few quotes to inspire you:

> *"Re-set, re-adjust, re-start, re-focus as many times as you need to."*
> —Zig Ziglar

> *"Make each day your masterpiece."*
> —John Wooden

FEEL GOOD X

ABOUT BHADA SINHAPHALIN

A native of Bangkok, Bhada Sinhaphalin worked for 23 years in the hospitality industry, including 19 years with Shangri-La Hotels and Resorts in Thailand, Malaysia, China, Singapore, and Hong Kong, where he rosed to Hotel Manager and two years with Dusit International in Thailand where he was General Manager and Area Director.

During his highly competitive and stressful career, Bhada changed his diet and turned to meditation and exercise to improve his wellbeing. At 52, he had the epiphany that career success, even along with proper diet and meditation, was not the only path to a happier and better life. He, then, decided to search for a new way and learned many new skills, including attending the Functional Nutrition Guide training bymindbodygreen.com, where he earned the mbgFNG Certificate. He also completed the one year course successfully for certification as a Health Coach from New York's Institute for Integrative Nutrition and enhanced his knowledge by learning NLP and qualified as Practitioner of NLP (Neuro-Linguistic Programming) Coaching and Time Line Therapy.

He is now the creator of FeelGoodX, a movement, and a community dedicated to helping people live their best lives. FeelGoodX includes the elements essential to infuse higher levels of joy and satisfaction into life. Food is a part of one's approach to overall health and wellbeing, but it must be accompanied by good emotional health, financial security, purpose, mindset and practice, body and movement, home environment, and relationships. All these factors combined form the wheel of useful life and excellent health.

Bhada and his family live in Bangkok.

FEELGOODX
LIVE YOUR LIFE, LOVE YOUR LIFE

Acknowledgements

First and foremost, I want to thank you, the reader. This is my first book, so a big thank you for your confidence in my work!

The world is a better place thanks to people who want to guide and lead others. What makes it even better are people who share the gift of their knowledge to mentor or lead someone like me. Thank you to everyone who strives to grow and help others grow through various means. They continue to inspire me and give me a good foundation. It is the educational version of *The Lion King* song, "Circle of Life."

Without the one-year course from the Institute of Integrative Nutrition and the Functional Nutrition Guide certification course by mindbodygreen.com, this book would not exist. Both courses have given me the opportunity to gain proper knowledge. Although this period of my life was filled with many ups and downs, my time in these studies was worth it, and my experiences as a health coach have been memorable.

Having an idea and turning it into a book is as hard as it sounds. The experience is both internally challenging and rewarding. Writing a book is harder than I thought and more rewarding than I could have ever imagined. I especially want to thank the individuals who helped make this happen. Complete thanks to Chantel Hamilton who has an indisputable talent for improving my manuscript to resonate with the reader. She made my writing sound like me, only better! Her ability to understand what is important makes her a profoundly effective editor. My manuscript needed her, and I'm grateful that I found her.

I am grateful for Robert Boxwell, a longtime friend who helps me with whatever I need and who also led me to Melinda Yew, a super talented lady who is an amazing graphic artist and has been working with me on multiple projects for years. I appreciate her meticulous work on this book's interior and all the infographic charts.

Thanks to Diana Khoo, another longtime friend who recommended I contact Raman Krishnan of Silverfish Books, my publisher. Raman guided me all along and answered my never-ending questions. He is such a pleasure to work with!

Lastly, I want to thank my wife, Evelyn. She is the one who has to put up with me. She does so with love and patience instead of strangling me. I try to let her know how much I appreciate her as often as I can. This is me letting the rest of you know, too. You have this book because of her, as she is the one who inspired me years ago to pursue my interest in improving wellbeing and feeling good. Thank you, Evelyn, for your love and support.

About the book cover

The color magenta is one of universal harmony and emotional balance. For psychology, magenta represents universal love at its highest level. It promotes compassion, kindness, and cooperative and encourages a sense of self-respect and contentment in those who use it.*

There is also pink in this cover. The pink color stands for unconditional love and understanding and undertaking and associated with giving and receiving care. Pink is also a sign of hope. It is a positive color that inspires warm and comfortable feel.**

Let both colors inspire you to the inner world of FeelGoodX.

John Yap designed the cover. He is a long-time friend from Penang, Malaysia.

Sources:
* www.empower-yourself-with-color-phychology.com
** www.color-meanings.com